This I Believe

CHARLES T. CRABTREE

Radiant BOOKS

Gospel Publishing House/Springfield, Mo. 65802

02-0758

The Statement of Fundamental Truths is not intended to cover all points of doctrine taught by the
Assemblies of God. However, the truth contained
therein is held to be essential to a full-gospel ministry.
In this book, sections 2 and 10 of the Statement are not
quoted in their entirety.

©1982 by the Gospel Publishing House, Springfield, Missouri
65802. All rights reserved. No part of this book may be
reproduced, stored in a retrieval system, or transmitted in any
form or by any means, electronic, mechanical, photocopy,
recording, or otherwise, without prior written permission of the
copyright owner, except brief quotations used in connection with
reviews in magazines or newspapers.

Library of Congress Catalog Card Number 81-84913
International Standard Book Number 0-88243-758-5
Printed in the United States of America

Contents

1

You'd Better Believe It!

The Scriptures Inspired

The Scriptures, both the Old and New Testaments, are verbally inspired of God and are the revelation of God to man, the infallible, authoritative rule of faith and conduct (2 Timothy 3:15-17; 1 Thessalonians 2:13; 2 Peter 1:21).

Most churches have a constitution and bylaws. To most people that statement is about as interesting as the address of the I.R.S. However, all reasonable people know the necessity of clearly defined guidelines to avoid unnecessary conflict.

In addition to a recognized man-made constitution and bylaws, a church also adopts a spiritual constitution and bylaws called the "tenets of faith." Simply stated, the tenets of faith are statements of belief. Although written by men, they are recognized as the basic divine truths that are individually and collectively believed by a given church.

The tenets of faith are *what* we believe. But *why* we believe them is even more vital. The purpose of this book is to explain the reasons behind the tenets of our faith.

Our church has 16 tenets, or anchors, of faith. The first one concerns the Bible. We accept the Holy Scriptures as the revealed will of God, the all-

4

sufficient rule for faith and practice. There are several reasons for our belief in this first tenet of faith.

Divine Origin and History

We believe the Bible is the inspired Word of God because of its divine origin and history. From the testimony of Scripture itself, we learn in 2 Peter 1:21 that holy men spoke as they were inspired or moved upon by the Holy Spirit. Second Timothy 3:16 tells us all Scripture is given by the inspiration of God. Over and over, Jesus testified to the divine inspiration of the Scriptures. In John 5, He states that they hold eternal life and testify of Him. Psalm 119:89 declares the Word of God is settled in heaven. The Bible ends with a warning: we are not to tamper with the Holy Scriptures by adding to or taking away from them.

Many centuries ago, the church recognized the Books of the Bible as inspired through the canon of Scripture. The word *canon* literally means "a measuring rod." Sacred writings were put to the test, and only the Books of the Bible met the criteria of the canon without question.

The canon of Scripture has five guiding principles: (1)Is it authoritative? Does the book give unquestionable evidence of being divinely inspired? Did it come from God? (2)Is it authentic? Has the authenticity of the writing been confirmed without question? (3)Is it prophetic? Does it have truth beyond the ability of the mind of man at the time of its writing? (4)Is it dynamic? Does it manifest life-transforming power to the individual who reads its pages? (5)Is it universally accepted by the people of God as being the inspired Word of the Lord?

Down through the centuries, God placed a holy desire in the hearts of His people to carefully preserve the Scriptures. One of the reasons God chose to bless the nation of Israel was for the purpose of guarding the Holy Scriptures. Israel recognized the inspired Scriptures and jealously protected every word. Protection of the Scriptures was a national passion. The most trusted and learned Jewish scholars were assigned the task of meticulously copying the Scriptures from the original manuscripts.

Many times worldly kingdoms and hostile dictators threatened to destroy the Holy Scriptures, but in spite of their hatred and animosity, God always found a way to miraculously preserve the Bible. Today our church recognizes the Holy Bible as its single most important possession, inseparable from the living God himself.

Internal Evidence

We believe the Bible is the inspired Word of God because of its internal evidence. The Bible is miraculous in its unity.

For a moment, let us imagine that God had nothing to do with the Bible. Here is the task: man is going to produce a book with 40 different authors. The book will span over 1,500 years in time. (This means that if the book were to be published in the year A.D. 2000, the first writings would have had to have been started in A.D. 400.) The book will be written in three languages by men from as varied professions as that of a shepherd, a king, a soldier, a doctor, a tax collector, and a farmer. At the same time, there must be a continuity without collusion, and the authors must speak out on every major moral subject without contradicting each other.

Imagine people from varied walks of life writing a book without collaboration and without any major conflicts! We can only come to one conclusion: although the building of God's Word, line upon line, took well over 1,000 years, there was only one Architect who put all the pieces together. Under the guidance of the Holy Spirit, men were inspired to each add a part until we were given the complete revelation of the written Word of God.

The prophetic accuracy of the Bible points to an important internal evidence. We are not discussing a good percentage of accuracy, but 100-percent accuracy. The Bible meets the most stringent tests of prophecy. We will consider a few in the following paragraphs.

Remoteness of Time. There must be such a separation between the prediction and its fulfillment that the prophet can have no power, directly or indirectly, to influence the result. This criteria is met over and over again in the Bible's prophecies concerning Israel, the nations, and Christ.

Is it by chance that the prophet Daniel predicted five historical worldwide Gentile powers when he was living in the second great world empire? Is it mere speculation that Micah, a shepherd, was able to predict the village in which the Messiah would be born 400 years before the event? How could Ezekiel have understood what he was writing when he foretold the present coalition of nations just before the coming of Christ (Ezekiel 38; 39)? How did the prophets know Israel, with its God-given blessings, would be destroyed and the seed of Abraham scattered throughout the whole earth? And how could they have known that in the latter times it would become a nation again?

Most of our modern seers have a hard time with next week, let alone with the next millennium. But the One who wrote the Word of the Living God has no problem with time, because a thousand years are as a day with Him.

Minuteness of Detail. Another test of prophecy demands that the prediction's details be so many and minute that it cannot be attributed to blind luck or shrewd guesswork. For instance, the most critical student would be overwhelmed by the details of prophecy concerning Israel, but equally astounding are the prophecies concerning the nations surrounding Israel. There were 12 major countries in or near Israel's borders in Old Testament times. Years in advance, the prophets accurately predicted the future of each of these countries. Minor details, such as who would conquer them and how it would be done, were foretold.

In one prophecy concerning Babylon, the prophet Isaiah's prediction of a siege included this detail: "Two things shall come to thee in a moment in one day, the loss of children, and widowhood" (Isaiah 47:9). In the midst of that siege, and driven to madness by famine, the Babylonians strangled 50,000 of their women and children in one day, sparing only enough to bake bread during the siege.

The minute details of Christ's life, as prophesied in the Scriptures, defy the random chance theory so completely that any objective student must conclude that Biblical prophecy is divine. There are hundreds of prophecies concerning Christ; covering 61 major areas of His life. One must realize these prophecies were given hundreds of years before the actual events. The latest Old Testament prophecy concerning Jesus was given over 400 years before its fulfillment.

The prophecies concerning Christ include such details as His virgin birth, the village of Bethlehem where He would be born, and that He would be presented with gifts by kings of Sheba. They also predict His ministry of miracles, His use of parables, His betrayal by a friend for 30 pieces of silver (which would be thrown or cast down in God's house), His crucifixion with thieves, and the casting of lots for His garments. These are just a few of the intricate details prophesied hundreds of years before the events occurred.

Novelty of Combination. A further test of prophecy demands there be nothing in previous history that would make it possible to forecast a similar event in the future. There must be something new in the combination. The prophecy of a king being born of a virgin in a small village, being called out of Egypt, and growing up to be called a Nazarene is certainly a novel combination beyond the wildest imaginations of man. Who would think of a king on a cross, or the metaphors of a lamb and a lion being applicable to the same individual?

In my opinion, the present alignment of nations in the Middle East brings into focus the veracity and inspiration of the Scriptures. The alliances of politics are usually destroyed within a millennium, but to think a mere mortal could predict the complex coalitions of future governments, as described in Ezekiel 38 and 39, defies simple logic.

Clearness of Forecast. Prophecies must not be ambiguous, as many current-day ones are. When the event occurs, there must be no question as to its original prediction.

Biblical prophecy is not ambiguous. For instance, in Jeremiah 51:31 there is a prophecy concerning the fall of Babylon. The prophet said messengers would run to and fro to inform the king of the invasion by Cyrus, and later predicted the opening of the gates from within. The Babylonians were occupied with their merriment when Cyrus advanced. He struck both sides of the city simultaneously. The startled messengers ran for the palace and met each other midway. The people were so dismayed, they opened the great gates to the invader!

Scientific Knowledge. Another proof of inspiration is the scientific knowledge of Scripture, which was far beyond the ability of the writers. Moses certainly did not know the chemical composition of man, yet he correctly wrote that God made man from the dust of the ground. How could Jeremiah have known of the vast number of the stars? The ancients had catalogued and named all existing stars visible to the human eye. In Jeremiah's time, less than 3,000 stars were known to man, and yet the prophet said: "As the host of heaven cannot be numbered, neither the sand of the sea measured . . ." (Jeremiah 33:22).

The ancients had no concept of the immensity of space. They supposed the earth to be stationary within a solid sphere. But Jeremiah knew differently. He said: "If heaven above can be measured, and the foundations of the earth searched out beneath, I will also cast off all the seed of Israel" (Jeremiah 31:37). While men assault the Bible, the world and the universe ring out a message of confirmation; pealing forth their anthems of praise to Him.

10

Moral Power and Influence

Finally, we believe the Bible is inspired because of its moral power and influence. No other book has had such an impact on nations and individuals. The Church has continually thrilled to the supernatural results seen in those who believe and stand upon the Bible. In a day when men have lost their spiritual moorings and are floundering on the slippery slopes of doubt, God has provided an anchor that will never move.

One of the areas of concern in some institutions is a debate over the inspiration, infallibility, and inerrancy of Scripture. My fear as a pastor is that some will lose the practical power of scriptural authority while crossing *t*s and dotting *i*s. In so doing, it is possible to become so concerned about the declarations of men regarding the Word of God that the Word itself is lost.

The Bible still stands as the inspired, inerrant Word of God. The magnifying glass of the skeptics has not revealed any structural flaws; no errors of design have been discovered. Those who have trusted in the Word have winged their way to glory. If God Almighty has declared this vehicle to be the infallible truth in which we can put all our trust, then we must convey its message to as many people as possible.

I would love to see a new respect for apologetics and scholastic achievement anointed by the Holy Spirit, whereby Spirit-filled technicians would continually examine the Bible for the purpose of defending it as the inspired, inerrant, and infallible Word of God, and not for the purpose of questioning its integrity.

God's Word is without error, but man has erred in

his handling of it. There have been some printers' mistakes, but God has protected His Word. There has been no design or structural damage that in any way affects the integrity of the Word of God. I appeal to Bible scholars to use all their God-given wisdom and insight to strengthen the pulpit by confirming the Word and not in any way questioning its integrity.

If the Word is completely trustworthy (and to affirm otherwise is heresy), then the task of Bible scholars and students is to strengthen the veracity of the Word through academic pursuits, not drawing attention to the scholars themselves, but to their Saviour.

Some time ago, a party of mountain climbers met with an accident on a sheer cliff. The lowest man in the party of five lost his balance and pulled down another man with him; then he, in turn, pulled down two others. All lost their hold except the leader, who had such a grip on the rock that he was able to hold on long enough for the man below him to regain his hold. The other men followed likewise, until finally they all were saved.

In these times of trouble and moral earthquakes, you will never be confounded or brought to shame if you will cling with tenacious passion to our first anchor of faith—the inspired, infallible, and inerrant Word of God. Not only will you be saved, but also others who follow you will be stabilized and know the security of Bible bedrock upon which all doctrine is based.

2

Man! What a God!

The One True God

The one true God has revealed himself as the eternally self-existent "I Aᴍ," the Creator of heaven and earth, and the Redeemer of mankind. He has further revealed himself as embodying the principles of relationship and association as Father, Son, and Holy Ghost (Deuteronomy 6:4; Isaiah 43:10,11; Matthew 28:19; Luke 3:22).

"The fool hath said in his heart, There is no God" (Psalm 14:1). In spite of all the denials of atheism and the doubts of agnosticism, there are comparatively few fools. Most men believe in some kind of a Supreme Being.

We believe God exists. Books are full of arguments for the existence of God. Most of them are aimed at the head instead of the heart, but many of them miss the mark and go over the head!

Reasons for Believing in God

We believe in God for good, sound reasons. The first reason we call *First Cause*. Because there is balance and design, and natural laws and consistency, in our world, we conclude there is a designer, a cause behind the effect. It would be as foolish to say there is no designer behind our complicated and intricate world as to say there is no designer in the making of a TV set.

One day an artist finished a masterpiece in the presence of a colleague. "Aren't you going to sign it?" asked the friend. "No," said the master, "I sign it every time I put my brush to the canvas."

We know there had to be a designer behind this incredible universe. Everywhere we look, we are impressed by God's signature on His handiwork.

Another reason we believe in the existence of God is called the *moral argument*. There is a permanent moral law which holds great and impartial influence over us. Our conscience is not self-imposed because often our sense of moral duty is in conflict with our own desires and pleasures. Our conscience insists there is a fundamental, moral law in the universe and it is our duty to observe it. When we do not, we experience fears of judgment and soul unrest. We must conclude that since moral law is not self-imposed, there is a holy will and power, a great lawgiver, an ultimate authority—a living God.

Another reason we believe in the existence of God is called the *argument from congruity*. This is just another way of saying that the existence of a living, all-powerful God is the only key that fits the lock to the mystery of the universe. It best explains the facts of our mental, moral, and religious nature, as well as the facts of the material universe.

This argument is used in the science of astronomy. For instance, a man named Percival Lowell noticed certain variations in the motion of the planet Neptune. He concluded there must be another large body in that region of the universe. Careful study with powerful telescopes of that part

14

of the heavens led to the discovery of the planet Pluto in the year 1930.

Atheism leaves us with no key and no answers, but the child of God holds the key of revelation. Jesus, the visible and physical revelation of God, said, "I hold the keys." We are at the heart of the secret: we can be assured there is a God. Most people do not wrestle with the fact of God's existence, but rather with knowing for certain what kind of God exists.

Some people are atheists; they do not believe there is a God. Others are pantheists; they believe that God is all, and all is God. According to them, there is no distinction between God and the universe because the universe is God. Millions have been deists: they believe God wound up the world like a mechanical toy and turned it loose. But God has been seeking throughout the centuries to smash that theory.

Let us imagine Moses standing in astonishment before the burning bush. He draws near and hears a voice. God has come—Israel's God—who has become only a vague memory. Thundering from out of the bush come powerful words of revelation: "I AM THAT I AM" (Exodus 3:14). "Moses, I am not a distant drummer, or a cold, unfeeling genius. I am a Person; I am One. I have heard the groanings of your people, and I have come down to deliver them."

So God is a Person; He is a Spirit-Person. Therefore, we must not insist on the same type of proof for God's existence as we demand for the existence of material things. This is a point so often missed in our striving to prove the existence of God to ourselves and others. *Our conviction of God is a faith,* not a science or a philosophy.

15

I am not implying that the object of our faith is uncertain, but the *processes* we use to prove the spiritual must differ from the processes used to prove the material universe. In knowledge, we verify something through investigation, argument, and proof. But faith is the vision of the Spirit that sees and hears its spiritual object. By faith, we understand the worlds were framed by the Word of God (Hebrews 11:3). Faith is the bond that unites us to the object of our faith.

This was the experience of Moses. He had been schooled in all the wisdom of Egypt. He had learned the Law and had been taught the precepts of Israel's God. But a person will never be transformed by someone else's God—he will only be changed by a *personal* God.

Moses had believed in a Spirit-Person God, but at the burning bush he met a present, personal God and, from that moment, Moses was a changed person.

Many centuries later, a man named Thomas, full of doubt and unbelief, lived in the presence of Jesus Christ, God clothed in the flesh. But Thomas was not changed until he moved past the material to the spiritual, from form to faith, and cried, "My Lord and my God" (John 20:28).

Until a person moves beyond a belief in a cold, calculating God who is to be avoided rather than sought, any further knowledge is impossible because the carnal or physical mind can only accept concrete, physical proof. The mind of man by itself cannot understand the evidence of the Spirit.

Characteristics of God

Let us examine some of the characteristics of God:

(1)God is self-existent. We are all dependent on something outside ourselves for our existence. But God has the ground of existence in himself. (2)God also has the dimension of immensity. He is not limited by space; in fact, all space is dependent on Him. (3)God is also eternal. He is not dependent on time, but rather, He is free from the succession of time in that He is the *cause* of time.

We have hardly begun to mention the wondrous attributes of our God. We believe He is present everywhere (Psalm 139:7-12). "He is not far from each one of us," Luke writes (Acts 17:27, RSV). The thought of His presence is encouraging to the believer, but a restraint and warning to the unbeliever.

We believe He is all-knowing. Scripture supports the truth that He who created all things knows all things. The Psalmist says: "His understanding is infinite" (Psalm 147:5). Hebrews 4:13 says there is no creature that is not manifest in His sight. The Bible abounds with the truth that the knowledge of God fills the earth. The very hairs of our head are numbered, and every sparrow is known by Him (Luke 12:6,7). He has numbered the host of heaven and has written all our names in the palms of His hands (Isaiah 49:16). We believe He knows the future. Man calls this foreknowledge, but to God it is simultaneous intuition. He who wrote prophecy is not surprised by what a day brings forth.

We believe our God is all-powerful. He can do all things except that which is contrary to His nature, for with God all things are possible. His power is expressed in His Word, called "the word of his power" (Hebrews 1:3). He has power to speak, and at that moment the entire universe is subject to His will and comes into conformity. Having all power is not the same as exercising that power; it is the *capability*. God has not chosen to keep sin out of the world by force. He has willed to limit His power in the face of free will.

We believe our God is unchanging—the same yesterday, today, and forever: "I am the Lord, I change not" (Malachi 3:6). He is perfect, so any change would make Him less than perfect. He is the one constant; all the change we see is outside of God. His responses to us may sometimes appear to change, just as our rotating earth gives the illusion to the earthbound that the mighty sun moves to rise and set each day. In the same manner, the limited and ignorant suppose God will change His nature and moral law. In this they are deceived. The mighty God changes not, though the earth whirls and the heathen rage.

But there is more. We have not yet spoken of God's moral attributes. The fact is, He is absolutely holy and separate from evil and sin. He is just; He never makes a mistake in His treatment of all the creatures in the universe. God is good; He is full of love and mercy. He is truth; He cannot lie. What a God!

Results of Believing in God

Believing in God causes practical differences in the life of the believer. Modern man is insecure. We have never had more things, yet the fear of loss takes away the joy of possessions. We are sitting on a political powder keg. Social insecurity abounds, and broken homes are becoming the norm instead of the exception. White collar crime invades the executive suite, and alcoholism and drug addiction have become a national shame.

Modern man is lonely, even though there is plenty of togetherness. The traffic jams on the highways are symbolic of the way lives are jostled until there is little time to be alone with one's thoughts. Yet few people feel really understood, and fellowship in the deepest sense is infrequent. Everywhere men are unloving. There is an increase in sexual activity, but a decrease in unselfish love. Love is longed for, sung about, and spoken about, yet men are cruel, defensive, hateful, and filled with spite. Where is God in this rat race? Who can save insecure, lonely, and unloving man?

Thank God, He has provided the answer for the longing of man's heart. First, God speaks to our insecurity. God is the creative and sustaining power at work in all creation. He is Lord of history. There is no circumstance so dark that He cannot redeem it.

God also speaks to our loneliness. God is a Person. Although He transcends our limited human personalities, we are made in His spiritual likeness. He knows us. Through Christ, God has found a way to establish a meaningful relationship. Through the avenue of prayer, we have communion with God. Jesus said, "Lo, I am with you alway" (Matthew 28:20). God has made it possible for us to have a never-ending companionship with Him. And we can have fellowship with His body through the Spirit.

God also speaks to our desire to be loved. God is love. He loves every man and yearns for his salvation and perfection. Above all other attributes, Jesus trumpeted the fact of God's love. This is our great assurance.

19

God condemns our sins, but He does not reject us. Mercy—not judgment—is God's final word. We have turned away from God, but He has never turned away from us.

Towering over the wrecks of time stands an old rugged cross. Here is the final proof: God so loved the world that He gave His best, so we could have His best.

3

Jesus—God With a Face

The Deity of the Lord Jesus Christ

The Lord Jesus Christ is the eternal Son of God. The Scriptures declare: (a)His virgin birth (Matthew 1:23; Luke 1:31,35). (b)His sinless life (Hebrews 7:26; 1 Peter 2:22). (c)His miracles (Acts 2:22; 10:38). (d)His substitutionary work on the cross (1 Corinthians 15:3; 2 Corinthians 5:21). (e)His bodily resurrection from the dead (Matthew 28:6; Luke 24:39; 1 Corinthians 15:4). (f)His exaltation to the right hand of God (Acts 1:9,11; 2:33; Philippians 2:9-11; Hebrews 1:3).

There are three basic schools of thought about Jesus Christ. The first school *denies* Him. "There was no Jesus," this view says. "He is the myth of Christendom, conceived not by the Holy Ghost, but by overactive and zealous minds."

When faced with the incredible and supernatural, it is the easiest thing in the world to deny it. In fact, it is so easy, most logical people fall into this trap. It is humbling for clever men to accept anything by faith. But when they refuse to do so, they carry the awesome burden of explaining the mysteries of life and taking the place of God. As hard as they try, Jesus will not go away. He *was* there; His story proves that. And He *is here*—a powerful, present reality still shaping the concepts and lives of men. To deny Him is to deny reality.

When a person denies Christ, he has problems. To be fair, he must deny Socrates, Plato, Caesar, Paul, and the pharaohs. He must find an explanation for the motivation behind some of the world's greatest literature, art, and music. He must explain why Christ's followers laid down their lives, and why His deathless words are so relevant in the 20th century. No! It makes no sense to deny the reality of Jesus Christ.

If it is implausible to deny Him, then one of the other two schools of thought must be accepted. The second view tries to *explain* Him in terms of human reasoning. Religious and intellectual pride recoil at denying Him. Yet to explain Him in strictly human terms is even more difficult.

The popular view of Christ says: "Let's not worry about the Virgin Birth; it's a side issue. Actually, it's an offense to man's pride. Now if you won't press the Virgin Birth, we can all agree that Jesus was a great man. His teachings were glorious, and His death was a beautiful example. We do have trouble with the Resurrection (there's that problem with the supernatural again). But, oh yes, we believe He lives. He lives in the thoughts and hearts of millions of His followers."

No! This view is not tenable either. The Scriptures declare Christ's virgin birth, so if you deny it, you have denied the Scriptures. If Jesus is a great man to you, but He is not the great God, you have taken the same position as the Jews who picked up stones to kill Him! Why? Because He made himself equal with God. To stone Him is more logical than letting Him live as a liar, imposter, or deranged fool. Jesus stood before the Jews in that moment as He stands before every unbelieving, proud, and self-righteous person. He is an offense, standing in the way of human wisdom.

Our church belongs to the third school of thought concerning Jesus Christ. We *accept* Him. We readily admit that we were all "doubting Thomases" at one time, but now we confess with Thomas, bowing before Him and crying aloud: "My Lord and my God" (John 20:28). There is no other explanation. We have good reasons for our belief, but even when reason has fled the scene, "our faith still holds and grips the solid rock."

The Deity of Jesus Christ

We accept the deity of the Lord Jesus Christ for several reasons. First, there are the claims of Scripture. God's Word has never led us astray. The Bible explains the great mysteries of life, but its main message concerns Jesus. The Holy Spirit inspired the Scriptures. Jesus came to fulfill the Scriptures. Who knows more about God than God himself? We are standing before a great and wondrous mystery, yet the Scriptures provide a look behind the curtain to all who will believe.

The man, Jesus of Nazareth, is the eternal God with a face. John declares it powerfully: "In the beginning was the Word, and the Word was with God, and the Word was God. The same was in the beginning with God. . . . And the Word was made flesh, and dwelt among us" (John 1:1,2,14). Colossians 1:16,17 states:

> By him were all things created, that are in heaven, and that are in earth, visible and invisible, whether

23

they be thrones, or dominions, or principalities, or powers: all things were created by him, and for him: and he is before all things, and by him all things consist.

Every page in the New Testament directly and indirectly glows with the deity of Jesus Christ. If we deny the deity of Christ, we deny the Scriptures.

We believe Jesus is divine because of His own claims. No other *credible* religious leader has ever claimed what Jesus claimed. Their writings say: "I am nothing in myself. My name may perish, but the message will live on." But Jesus claimed not merely to have found the truth, but to *be* the Truth: "I am the way, the truth, and the life: no man cometh unto the Father, but by me" (John 14:6). Jesus claimed to be greater than Solomon and Abraham (Matthew 12:42; John 8:58). He claimed to be God: "He that hath seen me hath seen the Father" (John 14:9).

We believe Jesus is divine because of His sinless life. His enemies turned the searchlight on His life, but with all their searching they never found a flaw in His character. Holy men throughout the ages have been known for their consciousness of their sins. Their writings are filled with statements of unworthiness, yet Jesus said: "Which of you convicts me of sin?" (John 8:46, RSV).

He was tempted in all points as we are, yet was without sin (Hebrews 4:15). He did no sin, neither was guile found in His mouth. Even when He was brought before Pilate to be examined, Pilate's verdict was: "I find no fault in him" (John 19:6).

We believe Jesus is divine because He did things that only God could do. He forgave sins. No one in Galilee or anywhere else had the authority to forgive sins. When the scribes questioned His authority, Jesus' answer was powerful: "Is it easier to say ... Thy sins be forgiven thee; or to say, Arise, and take up thy bed, and walk?" (Mark 2:9). Then He showed them: "That ye may know that the Son of man hath power on earth to forgive sins, ... I say unto thee, Arise, and take up thy bed, and go thy way into thine house" (Mark 2:10,11). And who else could meet the adultress and have the power to say, "Go, and sin no more" (John 8:11)?

Jesus did things *to men* that only God could do. Blindness was no match for Him—Bartimeus was proof of that. Paralysis could not stop Him—the man by the pool of Bethesda experienced that. Leprosy was defeated by Him—the 10 lepers experienced that, although only one returned to thank Him. A fever was no obstacle for Him—Peter's mother-in-law testified to that. Death was no match for Him—Jairus' daughter and Lazarus, who had been dead for 4 days, were living proof of that.

Jesus did things to nature that only God could do. Who else walked on the waves of Galilee? Only He who is Lord of heaven and earth. Jesus cursed a fig tree, and it never again bloomed. He told Peter to go fishing and he would find a coin in the mouth of a fish with which they could pay their taxes. He broke the bread and fish from a boy's lunch and fed a multitude. We accept the deity of Christ.

The Virgin Birth

We accept the incarnation of Jesus by the Virgin Birth. It is incomprehensible to think He would come into this world, wear a face, become a man, and taste sin for us. He must be God! He must be man!

He was sinless, yet He became sin. But how could these things be? Only through the power of the Holy Spirit. The answer will never be found in medical journals or in the wisdom of this world. You'll only find the answer by a living faith in the revealed truth of the Scriptures.

We believe in the Incarnation by the Virgin Birth because the Bible declares it, the angel announced it, and the prophet foretold it: "A *virgin* [not a *young woman,* as some translations dare interpret this] shall conceive, and bear a son" (Isaiah 7:14). The angel Gabriel came to Mary, the little virgin Jewess, and gently told her: "Mary, . . . you will conceive in your womb and bear a son, and you shall call his name Jesus. He will be great, and will be called the Son of the Most High; . . . and he will reign over the house of Jacob for ever; and of his kingdom there will be no end" (Luke 1:30-33, RSV).

Now Joseph had a problem. His fiancée was pregnant. He would have to put her away; it was the only natural thing to do. But Jesus had not been conceived naturally; He was supernatural. The angel of the Lord came to Joseph and mercifully explained the reason behind Mary's pregnancy: "Do not fear to take Mary your wife, for that which is conceived in her is of the Holy Spirit. . . . All this took place to fulfill what the Lord had spoken by the prophet: 'Behold, a virgin shall conceive and bear a son, and his name shall be called Emmanuel' (which means, God with us)" (Matthew 1:20,22,23, RSV).

A miracle now happened in Bethlehem. If someone had asked Joseph, "Why are you taking your wife, who is great with child, on this journey?" he probably would have replied, "Because Caesar Augustus decreed it." But a greater than Caesar had decreed it. Many years before, the Holy Spirit had moved a shepherd named Micah to declare that Jesus would be born in Bethlehem Ephratah.

Just about the time Mary conceived Jesus by the Holy Spirit, God moved the balance of payments and power of Rome, making it necessary for more taxes to be imposed. So Caesar Augustus decreed the whole world must be taxed, and God smiled. The Psalmist said: "Surely the wrath of man shall praise thee" (Psalm 76:10)—and there is no greater wrath of man than taxes! So, it was no trick at all to get Joseph and Mary to Bethlehem on time. All God had to do was shake up Rome's economy and make Caesar think he was the big shot!

So Jesus was born in a stable in Bethlehem. If we were to ask God why He chose such humble surroundings for Jesus' birth, He would probably answer, "Jesus came to destroy the sin that had destroyed the relationship between God and man—the sin of pride." Jesus was laid in a manger, so He could identify himself with the lowest among us. This God with a face was approached by kings and shepherds alike. He did not come to seek position or for those who had found themselves; He came to seek and to save that which was lost. If He had been born in a palace, only royalty would have felt free to touch Him. But the poor heard Him gladly; they knew all about it.

This is the God with a face. He dwelt among *us,* not them. He is the approachable God of Bethlehem's manger and Nazareth's carpenter shop. Because we accept His deity and virgin birth, we can believe everything He did, said, and promised.

Christ's Death and Resurrection

We believe He was crucified for the purpose of taking the sins of the world upon Him. Golgotha was not a mistake. Did you know the tragedy of Calvary was the triumph of the eternal God in disguise? Somebody had to die for our sins, and, until Jesus did, we were the ones who were under the curse of death and the power of sin. But when that Man on the cross—who was conceived by the Holy Spirit in the womb of the virgin Mary and declared to be the Son of God—cried, "It is finished" (John 19:30), He made it possible for us to be set free from the curse. Jesus said: "For this cause came I into the world" (John 18:37). He is the Lamb slain from the foundation of the world.

We believe He was buried and, on the third day, rose from the dead to complete the total victory over the grave. On the cross He defeated hell, but on the third day He defeated physical death. We believe that on the third morning following the Crucifixion, the clock of God's divine sovereignty struck the hour, and from heaven's Throne came a mighty command: "Now!" "And behold, there was a great earthquake; for an angel of the Lord descended from heaven and came and rolled back the stone, and sat upon it. His appearance was like lightning, and his raiment white as snow. And for fear of him the guards trembled and became like dead men" (Matthew 28:2-4, RSV).

Then the angel spoke to the women who had arrived at the tomb: "Do not be afraid; for I know that ye seek Jesus who was crucified. He is not here; for he has risen, as he said" (Matthew 28:5,6, RSV).

In John's vision on the Isle of Patmos, he saw the

conquering King of kings. And Jesus said: "I am he that liveth, and was dead; and, behold, I am alive for evermore, Amen; and have the keys of hell and of death" (Revelation 1:18).

We believe Jesus ascended on the 40th day after His resurrection and reentered the courts of heaven. Can you imagine the clamor and the worship as God the Father stood to welcome home His only begotten Son? At that moment, He gave Him a name that is above every name. But do you know what Jesus decided to do with all His power? He decided to become our High Priest in heaven's court. That is why you can go to Him with all your sins, and He will forgive you, that the Scriptures might be fulfilled.

The Second Coming

We believe He is coming again, according to the Scriptures. Nothing has stopped Him before. People have doubted His beginning, and they have denied the ending. But we believe His Word. God said: "This is my beloved Son, in whom I am well pleased; hear ye him" (Matthew 17:5).

On the basis of His Word, we confess Him as our Saviour and Lord. Because He lives, we live. Even if our body returns to mother earth, we will rise again at the sound of the last trumpet, that the Scriptures might be fulfilled (1 Corinthians 15:51-57).

I really feel God has put a love in my heart for trumpets. I'm waiting for Gabriel to finish his practicing. That is another promise: the trumpet *is* going to sound, that the Scriptures might be fulfilled. Maranatha!

4

Humpty Dumpty Had a Great Fall

The Fall of Man

Man was created good and upright; for God said,
"Let us make man in our image, after our likeness."
However, man by voluntary transgression fell and
thereby incurred not only physical death but also
spiritual death, which is separation from God
(Genesis 1:26,27; 2:17; 3:6; Romans 5:12-19).

"Humpty Dumpty sat on a wall. Humpty
Dumpty had a great fall." In untheological terms,
that's what happened to man. We were "sitting
pretty," and then the whole human race took a
shattering tumble. This chapter deals with the
intriguing story of man's high place and his great
fall.

To be honest, I hope I never hear another person
pose the questions: "Who am I?" "Where did I
come from?" "Where am I going?" You see, the
Christian faith has answered these questions so
clearly, that now they are redundant.

We believe man was created by God in the image
of God. We believe the Genesis account of man's
creation. But there are many well-meaning people
who don't believe the Bible, so they choose to live
with questions rather than answers.

Atheistic evolution tries to explain the origin and

nature of man in many ways. One way goes something like this: Once upon a time there was an explosion or disruption in the universe. A piece of a sun fell off (they don't tackle the problem of where that sun came from), and through another cosmic accident, this piece of sun was placed in orbit around another sun. Eventually it cooled down, and through a process of millions of years, the atmosphere and the earth were formed. Then, millenniums ago, a single-celled amoeba evolved in one of the oceans. Organic evolution caused a tail to be formed, allowing the amoeba to wiggle its way to a higher level of life. And, through the process of evolution and incredible mutations, the complex structures of all living creatures were formed.

When I read or hear the explanation of atheistic evolution, I can't help but think someone is trying to pull a good one on me!

We are not deistic evolutionists who teach that a Supreme Being designed the universe and set the evolutionary process into motion. Personally, I believe deistic evolution is less honest than atheistic evolution. Deistic evolutionists are pulling the same trick as those who tell us Jesus was a good, honest, and moral man—but He wasn't God.

If you are an evolutionist, you have to deny the scriptural account of creation. You place yourself in the position of telling God, "We know You didn't make us the way You said You did." Imagine the audacity of the creature second-guessing the Creator!

The Creation of Man

We believe the simple statement of the Scriptures

31

because God has never lied to us. It says: "In the beginning God created the heaven and the earth. . . . And the Lord God formed man of the dust of the ground, and breathed into his nostrils the breath of life; and man became a living soul" (Genesis 1:1; 2:7).

We have good reasons apart from Scripture to believe that we all came from one pair and one species. We have the argument from history. The evidence points to wave after wave of peoples and races coming from one common origin and ancestry in the Near East.

We have the argument from zoology which almost universally teaches monogenesis; that is, the species came from a single pair. It is interesting to note a statement of Charles Darwin's:

> It is interesting to note that the innumerable species, general and families, with which this world is peopled, are all descended, each within its own class or group, from common parents, and have all been modified in the course of descent, that I should without hesitation adopt this view, even if it were unsupported by other facts or arguments. (*Encyclopedia Britannica*, 1952 ed., s.v. "Darwin.")

We have the argument from linguistics which teaches that the rudiments of all languages can be traced to a single source.

We have the argument from physiology. If there is a process of evolution now going on, where can we see it in action? Where are the animals between the most advanced ape and the most retarded man? If the process of evolution is to be considered, we demand to know where ape-men now exist.

The evidence is irrefutable. The differences between the highest animal and the least-developed

32

human are so great, the rational mind is forced to conclude that man is the crowning act of a divine Creator and Designer. The differences between man and animal can be clearly seen in every cell of the body. Every human cell has 46 chromosomes, except for reproductive cells, which have 23. But where are the animals with 45 chromosomes in each cell? Where are the animals just below man in skeletal construction, in brain weight and activity, and in rationale and will? There are none, are there?

But more than all the arguments of science, and more than all the intellectual pursuits, we believe the ultimate authority of the universe: the Word of God. Genesis 2:7 states: "God formed man of the dust of the ground. . . ." Science has confirmed that the elements of which the human body is made are also found in the dust of the earth. "God . . . breathed into his nostrils the breath of life. . . ." So man was made of dust and breath. But there is more: ". . . And man became a living soul." Man is more than dust and breath; he is a soul. And with that soul made in the likeness of God, he rises to a place of dominion, authority, and complexity above all other creatures.

The Nature of Man

What then was the nature of man before his rebellion and sin? God said: "Let us make man in our image, after our likeness" (Genesis 1:26). The words *image* and *likeness* are used interchangeably. Mark 12:16 tells us that one day Jesus took a coin and asked the Pharisees and Herodians, "Whose is this image. . . ?" And they answered, "Caesar's." The coin was not Caesar's, but it belonged to him because his image was stamped on it. So God did not make little gods, but men—beings with His image stamped on them.

Obviously, we are not made in the *physical* likeness of God because God is pure Spirit. But we are made in the likeness of God in the nonphysical sense. Man is not primarily a body; he is primarily a soul, and soul is spirit. Because man is made in the image of God, he belongs to the same order of being as God himself, and his soul is eternal.

No animal has self-consciousness. No animal can sit down and speak of himself as "me." No animal can talk to himself and hold counsel with his inner self. Man, on the other hand, is able to reason in concept and carry through his reasoning to logical conclusions.

We are made in the moral likeness of God. We are made with a conscience and a will. If God wanted us to be like other animals, He would have made us with instincts alone, without the ability to reason and choose. But God placed His laws in our consciousness and gave us the ability to obey or disobey. There is a risk involved in having a child with a will of his own. It's scary. But when that child chooses to love and obey, it brings joy to the parents. Our will is the glory of man. God made man in His image with a will of his own because the risk was worth the pain.

We were made in the social likeness of God. Very few people realize the reason for which man was created. We are part of God's creation for the purpose of fellowship; we can know God and have things in common with Him.

Adam and Eve were perfect specimens of mankind—perfect in body, soul, and spirit. They were made to walk with God, to love God and each other, and to develop their world. But one day, man used his glory, his will, to rebel against God's authority. Man decided he didn't want to be in God's image anymore; he wanted *to be God.*

Satan tempted man: "God is not the authority —you are. Don't listen to Him." In that moment, man decided to become what *self* wanted to be, instead of being satisfied with what God intended him to be.

Here is the problem: All power belongs to God; there is no other real authority. So that Power has to be either obeyed or resisted. When Adam and Eve chose to rebel rather than obey, they entered a living death. With a free will they chose to be identified with a kingdom in rebellion against God. Several terrible things resulted. They lost their ability to have a meaningful relationship with God. The greatest fall in sin is the fall from friendship with God. No longer were they "insiders." They became "outsiders"; and, at that moment, *they were lost souls.*

The Nature of Sin

When something is made for a definite purpose, such as a typewriter, then its reason for being is the function for which it was created. But let us imagine the ribbon is taken out of the machine. The purpose of that typewriter can no longer be fulfilled. The person who uses it would be at a loss to know what to do with it. If the typewriter had self-consciousness and feeling, it would be hard pressed to explain its reason for being.

This is what happened to man. Man was made in the image of God to glorify God through obedience. But man rebelled and lost his "ribbon," and ever since the human race has tried to find fulfillment and meaning, but to little avail. *When a person loses his purpose, he loses his soul.* What does it profit a man if he gains the whole world and loses his purpose for being?

This is the nature of sin: it causes us to miss the mark, and our central purpose in life. We are programmed for eternity—a more integral plan than the space program. What happens to a spaceship when it rebels against the direction of the central command? It misses the mark. No matter how fine the aircraft, if it misses the mark, it is a failure.

Sin is a transgression of the law of God; it is disobedience to the divine Authority. Why does man choose to sin? Because he has lost his consciousness of God and chooses on the basis of what *seems* right, rather than what *is* right.

Because of Adam's sin, the human race was born with a nature of self-centeredness and rebellion against God. Man has a natural inclination to transgress God's law and live under the authority of Satan. This is expressed by selfishness. Thus, we are born in sin and "shapen in iniquity" (Psalm 51:5)—meaning, our moral nature is corrupt.

This does not mean that every sinner is void of all qualities pleasing to man. It means man has a spiritual *inability* to please God. He is destitute of love to God. He gives himself preference over the will of God and, by doing so, his sinful condition infects everything he does.

Because of Adam's sin, our whole world came under God's curse instead of His blessing. There was a time when the earth was a protectorate of the eternal God. Everything was kept under His guiding hand. But when Adam sinned, the earth was cursed. Thorns and thistles sprang up. The earth was separated from God's supernatural acts of blessing. The whole creation lost its original purpose, and now it groans under the weight of the Creator's displeasure.

All flesh was cursed. Because we were created to live forever, and because God could not allow man to continue in his physical state of sin, He brought the curse of physical death upon us to keep us from living forever in a rebel kingdom. Our bodies now are corrupt and mortal. Under Adam's sin, our souls are cursed—eternally existent, but eternally separated from our central purpose.

If you think Humpty Dumpty had a great fall, just look how far man fell. He fell from a place a little lower than the angels. Man had been given a perfect world and a perfect role, but in his selfishness he decided that all of God's blessings and God's laws were not enough.

This then is the nature of sin: We are surrounded by God's blessings, but we seek fulfillment outside the authority of God. We are confronted with God's law, but we decide to do what we want and ignore the sovereignty of God.

Men have taken their highest gift and glory, the right of free will, and instead of choosing God, they have chosen themselves. Let me urge you to call upon God; come back to the original purpose for which you were created. Find yourself by submitting to the authority of God.

God has a plan for every star and every atom. They are upheld by the word of His power. God has a plan for you, because man is the crown of creation. What a joy to know the Fall is not the end of the story, but merely the reason for the next chapter: the salvation of man.

5

But Somebody Can Put Humpty Dumpty Back Together Again!

The Salvation of Man

Man's only hope of redemption is through the shed blood of Jesus Christ the Son of God.

(a)Conditions to Salvation: Salvation is received through repentance toward God and faith toward the Lord Jesus Christ. By the washing of regeneration and renewing of the Holy Ghost, being justified by grace through faith, man becomes an heir of God, according to the hope of eternal life (Luke 24:47; John 3:3; Romans 10:13-15; Ephesians 2:8; Titus 2:11; 3:5-7).

(b)The Evidences of Salvation: The inward evidence of salvation is the direct witness of the Spirit (Romans 8:16). The outward evidence to all men is a life of righteousness and true holiness (Ephesians 4:24; Titus 2:12).

Humpty Dumpty had a great fall. And ever since, everybody has been trying to put Humpty Dumpty back together again, or pretending it never happened, or comparing Humpty with every other Dumpty and saying, "I'm okay, you're okay."

One school says, "Pull yourself together, Humpty." So Humpty tries, but after a while he realizes that all his efforts are in vain. He is still the same messed-up pile of fragmented junk he was after his fall from the wall.

Another school says, "You didn't mean to fall, so don't fight it." But Humpty knows the facts. In spite of all the kind words, his life is shattered, and he wants to become a whole, integrated person.

Another school says, "Let the king's horses and the king's men put you back together again." So the king's clerics, philosophers, psychiatrists, logicians, social workers, and legal experts go to work. But they can't put Humpty Dumpty back together again either.

Is there any hope? If all the king's horses and all the king's men can't put Humpty Dumpty together again, who can? Well, *the King can!*

The subject of this chapter is more important than any other subject. It is not just a matter of life and death; it is a matter of eternal life and eternal death. The message of salvation is called the "simple gospel," but it is a complex process. At the beginning of this book, we stated that *what* we believe is important. But *why* we believe is even more important. To understand this complex process, we will look at two views of the same subject: the divine perspective and the human perspective.

God's View of Sin

To understand the divine perspective we must understand God's view of sin. Only then can we know why God chose to go through the painful process of redeeming man. We must first understand God's righteousness. God loves man so much, but He hates sin with a divine passion.

Some time ago I was privileged to visit an operating room that was in the process of renovation. My doctor friend explained how the staff worked to keep the room sterile, free of germs.

He described a few of the precautions taken: a special filter system was used for temperature control, the instruments were sterilized by steam, and every person who entered the room wore sterilized coverings from head to toe.

To those who do not know or understand the unseen dangers of bacterial infection, these people would probably seem to be paranoid. Why the awesome precautions? Because those responsible had sworn to love man and save him from disease. On the other hand, they hated bacteria and infection because of their desire to help men in their need.

God created man morally clean. His soul was without the bacteria of sin. But when sin entered man's world through his disregard of sin's penalty, the contamination was passed along to all men, so that all men sin. God does not hate men; He loves them. But He hates sin so much that He cannot have any part with man in sin. Seen through His divine perspective, all good works are filthy. So God had to separate himself from us. He had no choice.

But man was made to be in fellowship with God. So how can we reestablish a meaningful relationship with God? What can we do to satisfy God's demands?

First, the Bible tells us there is no way we can satisfy the past. We are not equipped to meet the divine standard. Furthermore, there is nothing we own or have that can pay for the damage done. Second, God's law is the standard of conduct that must be lived up to in order to have fellowship. Even if we could enter the world of accountable actions without sin, or in perfection, if we broke one small part of God's law, we would be as guilty as if we had broken all of it.

What is the penalty for sin? God himself has rendered the verdict: Unless a way can be found to satisfy the demands of righteousness, God has no alternative but to pronounce the sentence of eternal separation upon all men, for all have sinned. Just as you would ban from an operating room any kind of filth, or a person who has a disease, God, in His love for righteousness, must ban all sin from His presence.

The consequences to men are tragic and devastating. If God holds such an impossible standard, and men cannot pay for their sin, there is no way. It is true that man has no way to put us back together with God, but God has provided a way.

God's Plan of Salvation

First, God had to devise a plan that would satisfy His law and at the same time enable sinful man to be free of the pollution of sin. He had to provide forgiveness and power. Since the penalty for sin is death, He provided a way whereby man could substitute another life for his own. Blood was shed, because the life of the flesh is in the blood (Leviticus 17:14). Only through the giving of a life by sacrifice could life be given.

We can view the plan of God in redemption throughout the Old Testament. Abel's sacrifice was accepted because blood was shed. Isaac was spared because a life was given and blood was shed. The Israelites were spared because the Passover lamb was slain. But the blood of bulls and goats was not enough to please God permanently. The sacrifices of the Old Testament were acceptable only as a temporary means. Man must die to satisfy the judgment on sin. Man, made in the image of God, had sinned, and he must die. Only God, *in the image of man,* could take man's place.

"For God so loved the world, that he gave his only begotten son" (John 3:16). Jesus Christ was the Lamb slain from the foundation of the world. He came, in the image of man, to give His life and shed His blood as the one sacrifice for sin. He was the only sacrifice whereby God could still be God—perfect in His law and uncompromising in His justice—and yet restore His fellowship with sinful men.

When a man cries "good works," God turns away in pain. But when a poor, sinful man cries, "Jesus!" God looks to see who has become His new friend.

Forgiveness, however, is not enough. To forgive past sins and leave the one who committed them still a sinner, is self-defeating. The sinner will sin in his next breath unless there is a new life principle. The forgiveness of sin makes it possible for God to *communicate divine life.* Through the creative Holy Spirit, a new nature is imparted to the sinner, which enables him to become a child of God through a new birth and gives him a new destiny by adoption into the spiritual family of God. At that moment, he is identified with and baptized into the body of Christ. He is brought into legal and spiritual union with God; becoming an heir of God and a joint heir with Jesus Christ.

From the divine side, the work is done. Man is forgiven through the blood of the Lamb. He is born again by the Spirit of God and is predestined through the foreknowledge of God to share in the kingdom of God forever.

But God does one further thing: He communicates His love for man through the agency of the Holy

Spirit. In the negative sense, He faithfully shows the sinner his desperate need of a Saviour and then reveals Christ's desperate desire to become that sinner's Saviour.

Too often people do not think of themselves as needing a savior because they do not understand that God judges them by His pure law in relationship to the glory of His holiness. All of us are quick to acknowledge bad sins or evil deeds and the need for punishment. But few realize that the good deeds applauded by men are considered evil and filthy when done in the glory of the flesh.

When a child does evil, establishing himself as an offender, he can do nothing good until the offense has been dealt with. In the same manner, God cannot approve or applaud any act of a man who has not been forgiven. All his "good" works are soiled and unacceptable because sin has not been forgiven on the divine level.

However, the Holy Spirit is faithful in revealing our sinful nature and showing us our spiritual death. How wretched we are! How sinful are our natures! But then the Holy Spirit comes to reveal Jesus as Saviour. God does not condemn us to damn us, but to save us.

Man's Part in Salvation

Now we are ready to consider the human perspective of our salvation. God has done all the work, taken all the action, and provided the means. Now it is man's responsibility to respond.

When looking at man's part in salvation, there are three words to remember: *repentance, faith,* and *obedience. Repentance* means a sincere and complete changing of the mind and disposition in regard to sin. It includes a sense of personal guilt and helplessness. This word is actually a positive word. Repentance is not negative, as many people think. While it is easily thought of as regret, remorse, and anguish, repentance is actually a turning around of the total person.

Repentance has an *intellectual* element. It involves a conscious change of view: seeing one's life in the light of God's truth, and understanding the state of one's soul. It is a knowledge born of the Spirit of God.

Repentance has an *emotional* element—a feeling of deep sorrow. As the Spirit of God awakens the individual to his sin, a sense of guilt sweeps over his whole being, and his emotions are stirred to move toward God.

Repentance has a *volitional* element. That is, we are given the right and ability to make a decision concerning what we have been, what we have done, and where we are going. In this sense, man is now responsible for his own salvation. We believe God's will is sovereign in the *means* of salvation. But we believe man's will is sovereign in his *acceptance* of that means.

The second word in salvation from the human side is *faith*. Faith is simply the ability to receive what we do not have and to do what we have not been able to do. The Bible says we are saved by faith in what Christ has accomplished by His work on Calvary.

Repentance qualifies us to receive Jesus Christ. Faith is the *ability* to receive Jesus Christ. "But as many as received him, to them gave he power to become the sons of God" (John 1:12). This is the point where Satan tries to block the sinner from receiving salvation. The sinner realizes his inability to receive Christ because of sin. The Holy Spirit must make him aware of his ability to receive Christ because of the Saviour's atoning work.

The third word in salvation from the human perspective is *obedience*. We believe in a continuing act of salvation. "If we walk in the light, as he is in the light, we have fellowship [as opposed to separation or death] one with another, and the blood of Jesus Christ his Son cleanseth [or keeps on cleansing] us from all sin" (1 John 1:7). We will understand this better after our discussion of sanctification (chapter 9), but suffice it to say we can willfully turn away from God, just as we can turn toward God in repentance.

Too many are looking only at the divine side, or the human side, and failing to blend the will and work of God with the free choice of man. But when you put them together, this is what happens: God made man with a free will—free to choose. Man chose sin. Because man chose to sin, God, who is holy, could have nothing to do with him. But God loved man, so He chose to find a way to forgive man of his sin and yet satisfy His holiness. God chose to send His only Son to earth to die, so man could find forgiveness. And God sent the Holy Spirit to reveal Jesus as man's Saviour.

Through the Holy Spirit, man chooses his Saviour. God, in His foreknowledge, knows who is going to choose His Son before the actual choice is made. Because God knows ahead of time, He declares that person saved. Just as we know faith is the evidence of things not seen, foreknowledge is the ability to know things before they occur. God then predestines each person who will choose His only begotten Son to become one of His sons. When the sinner chooses Jesus, God has already made provision. The sinner is forgiven and receives a new nature through the new birth. "Old things are passed away; behold, all things are become new" (2 Corinthians 5:17). God has made provision, the sinner accepts it, and that settles it!

Why do I believe Jesus saves? Because the Bible declares it, the Holy Spirit reveals it, and Christ has done it. Furthermore, I have personally experienced new life in Jesus.

I am reminded of something from my childhood that illustrates new life in Christ. I grew up in timber country. My native state of Maine has some of the greatest pulp mills in the world, and I often watched the miracle of papermaking. Big, old, ugly, dirty, and scarred logs were dumped into the channels and rivers leading to the mill. Then, through a short process, the logs became white sheets of paper.

> Come now, and let us reason together, saith the Lord: though your sins be as scarlet, they shall be as white as snow; though they be red like crimson, they shall be as wool (Isaiah 1:18).

Our old lives are scarred and ugly, but when we enter the channel of His love and submit to Him, the process of salvation makes us new creatures.

Humpty Dumpty fell a long way, and all the king's horses and all the king's men couldn't put him back together again. But incredible as it may seem, the King himself will put him back together if Humpty will ask Him. And He will do it for you too, if you will ask Him.

6

The Sacraments—
Dead Tradition or Living Truth?

Ordinances of the Church

(a)Baptism in Water: The ordinance of baptism by immersion is commanded in the Scriptures. All who repent and believe on Christ as Saviour and Lord are to be baptized. Thus they declare to the world that they have died with Christ and that they also have been raised with Him to walk in newness of life (Matthew 28:19; Mark 16:16; Acts 10:47,48; Romans 6:4).

(b)Holy Communion: The Lord's Supper, consisting of the elements—bread and the fruit of the vine—is the symbol expressing our sharing the divine nature of our Lord Jesus Christ (2 Peter 1:4); a memorial of His suffering and death (1 Corinthians 11:26); and a prophecy of His second coming (1 Corinthians 11:26); and is enjoined on believers "till He come!"

To many people, the ordinances have become a sacred tradition that must be protected at all costs, because our Lord commanded the Christian community to observe them. However, their observance is meaningless because it is merely vain repetition.

To others, observing the ordinances gives a feeling of spiritual achievement and helps them avoid a guilt trip. "Well there!" these people seem to say, "I've performed my spiritual duty. I don't understand what it's all about, but no one can point a finger at me!"

Still others couldn't care less if the ordinances were ever administered. They participate with everyone else only to avoid looking silly and raising questions.

These unfortunate responses grow out of a lack of teaching and real understanding. In this chapter, it is our goal to make participation in the sacraments meaningful and spiritually enriching.

Definitions

Our first task is to breathe life into some words that have died through neglect or misunderstanding. Augustus Strong, a brilliant theologian, has defined three important words for us.

A *symbol* is the visible representation of an invisible truth or idea. For instance, the lion is a symbol of strength and courage. The olive branch has become a symbol of peace. The wedding ring is a symbol of marriage, and foot washing was a symbol of the humility and service of our Saviour. So the two ordinances of our church are symbols. Water baptism is a symbol of our identification with Christ in His burial and resurrection. Communion is a symbol of our identification with Christ's death on the cross to provide salvation and healing.

A *rite* is a symbol that is used with regularity and sacred intent. An illustration of a sacred rite in our church is the laying on of hands at ordination. Using this definition, our ordinances (namely, water baptism and Communion) are rites because they are symbols employed by the church on a regular basis.

An *ordinance* is a symbolic rite that sets forth the central truths of the Christian faith and is a universal and perpetual obligation. Baptism and Communion have become ordinances by the specific command of Christ and by their relation to essential truth. No ordinance is a sacrament in the sense of conferring grace or salvation, but baptism and the Lord's Supper are sacraments in the sense that they are sacred vows of allegiance to Christ, our Master. The *sacramentum* was the oath taken by the Roman soldier to obey his commander, even unto death.

In essence, the ordinances are the acting out, or visual representation, of the essential truths of the gospel, as a means to display the grace of God, the work of Christ for our salvation, and our allegiance to Him before the Church and the world.

Water Baptism by Immersion

Let us turn our attention now to the ordinance of water baptism. Our church believes in and practices water baptism by immersion for many reasons. This ordinance was established by Christ by both His example and His command.

In Matthew 21:25-27, the Lord revealed the practice of Christian baptism as born of God, and not of man. He stated that John the Baptist's commission to baptize came not from men, but from heaven. In His own submission to baptism, He established the mode, or manner, and set baptism as an example to all believers.

He also directed His disciples to baptize, and this they did faithfully. In the Great Commission, Jesus made baptism an ordinance of universal obligation: "Go ye therefore, . . . baptizing them in the name of the Father, and of the Son, and of the Holy Ghost" (Matthew 28:19). This commission has never been repealed, and thus, is binding upon the church.

We believe in immersion and not sprinkling because of the example of our Lord and the pattern found in the New Testament. When Jesus was baptized, He came "up out of the water" (Mark 1:10)—setting our primary example. John 3:23 tells us that John the Baptist was baptizing in the area near Salim because there was *much water* there. If he was not baptizing by immersion, why would the writer have made a point of mentioning much water?

Philip, in baptizing the Ethiopian eunuch, very clearly demonstrated immersion as the New Testament pattern. The Bible emphasizes the fact that Philip and the eunuch came up out of the water (Acts 8:39).

The etymology of the word *baptism* is another reason we immerse. The meaning of the original word in the Greek is to immerse or dip. The Greek writers, including the church fathers, interpreted the command as a directive to immerse.

Still another reason we immerse is because of the symbolism of baptism. It is one of the most powerful and graphic testimonies of salvation. Baptism is a symbol of the death and resurrection of Jesus Christ. The power of the symbol, however, is found in the fact that we are directly identified with Christ through water baptism. We testify to the whole world that we believe in Christ's atoning death, which is our deliverance from the power of sin, and His subsequent resurrection.

Reasons for Water Baptism

Through water baptism we have the privilege of saying, "Look, I have faith in Jesus Christ to such an extent that what happened to Him has happened to me. From this moment on, I am identified with Christ's death; I am buried with Him. Through identification with His death, I further confess death to, and separation from, sin—a cutting away, or putting off, of the old life."

Paul says we are "circumcised with the circumcision made without hands, in putting off the body of the sins of the flesh by the circumcision of Christ: buried with him in baptism, wherein also [we] are risen with him" (Colossians 2:11,12). Paul is showing us how important baptism should be, in that it signifies "spiritual circumcision," or separation from the world.

Paul gives further meaning to water baptism:

> Know ye not, that so many of us as were baptized into Jesus Christ were baptized into his death? Therefore we are buried with him by baptism unto death: that like as Christ was raised up from the dead by the glory of the Father, even so we also should walk in newness of life (Romans 6:3,4).

In baptism, there is a dying to sin and a burial of the old. But, thank God, baptism also signifies resurrection. The old life is buried, but we are not to remain buried. We are made *alive* to God. We are raised from spiritual death to spiritual life, and now we have His resurrection life, eternal life, within us. Our new life is hid with Christ in God. "Old things are passed away; behold, all things are become new" (2 Corinthians 5:17).

Often we have looked on water baptism as just a duty, a command to obey, rather than as a privilege or an opportunity to declare allegiance to Christ and be identified with the Saviour in His work for us.

In most cultures, the act of Christian baptism is

the most definitive act a Christian can take. In some countries, a person risks his life by obeying the Lord and being baptized. In many religious cultures, any member of the family who identifies himself with the Christian faith is excommunicated. And in some cases, actual funerals are held for members of the family who dare to be publicly identified with the Christian faith by baptism.

Oftentimes, the things that are made easy are despised. In modern America, baptism has met with very little resistance or stigma. Thus, many Christians feel it is a nonbinding and even unnecessary act. However, we do not obey our Lord because it is easy or hard, popular or unpopular, convenient or inconvenient; we obey our Lord because *He is Lord.* No person has the right or privilege to countermand a command of his Commander-in-Chief.

We will soon appear before our Lord and the hosts of heaven, and before countless thousands who have had the honor and privilege of dying for their Christ because they followed Him in baptism. Will we dare to say to Him who gave His life for us: "Lord, I hope You'll understand, but I had a fear of water and I just couldn't bring myself to be baptized!" or, "Lord, I didn't want to get all wet in front of people!"?

Jesus said: "Anyone who is ashamed of me . . . , I, the Messiah, will be ashamed of him" (Mark 8:38, *The Living Bible*). No Christian can, with good conscience, justify noncompliance with a divine command. Instead, it would be better for new converts to invite a host of their unsaved friends to witness their baptism and afterward invite them to their home for a time of celebration. We should be like the young lad who came to his pastor after the announcement of a baptismal service and said, "I want to be advertised too!"

Errors Concerning Baptism

Now we will consider some errors surrounding baptism. We do not believe in baptismal regeneration. We teach baptism *because* we are saved, not *to* become saved. The power is in the Blood, not in the tub. The thief on the cross was redeemed, although not baptized, because it is Christ's finished work that saves: "By grace are ye saved through faith; and that not of yourselves: it is the gift of God" (Ephesians 2:8).

We do not believe in infant baptism for the following reasons: (1)Infant baptism is not expressed or implied in the Scriptures. (2)It is contradicted in the Scriptures. The Great Commission commands us to baptize only believers and disciples. (3)It is contrary to the very symbolism of baptism. You would not bury a person until he was dead. (4)Infant baptism teaches that an organic connection in the flesh has some means of grace. We are not saved by the flesh, but rather through believing faith in God. (5)It builds a false faith in a child and leads to false assumptions.

We do not believe in baptism for the dead. The only reference in Scripture to a baptism for the dead was made by Paul, and he used it as an argument to show the heathen that it was illogical for them to baptize for the dead (which was a heathen practice), if they didn't believe in the resurrection. We will be called to answer for the deeds done in *our* body, not someone else's.

We do not believe in multiple baptisms because

there is no record of second baptisms in the Scriptures, except where the individual had been baptized in ignorance or in false doctrine. Multiple baptisms would nullify the symbol of the perfect work of Christ.

The Importance of Communion

We now turn our attention to the ordinance or sacrament of the Lord's Supper. We commemorate the Lord's Supper as a sacred rite to show our continued dependence on the once-crucified and now risen Lord.

We practice this ordinance for several reasons. In the Gospels, we read that our Lord instituted the Lord's Supper by example. Prior to His death, He took time to show the disciples what He wanted them to do and what He wanted them to teach the Church in the years to come. Furthermore, there is an apostolic injunction to celebrate this rite until the Second Coming (1 Corinthians 11:26). It is a substitute for the Paschal Supper, to commemorate salvation by the Blood.

The fact that this ordinance was uniformly practiced by the New Testament Church and, in subsequent ages, by almost all churches who call themselves Christian, points to its vital importance. It has been an unbroken pattern of worship since the resurrection of Jesus Christ. It is one of the most glorious parts of Christian worship because it was divinely instituted and reminds us of God's love. If you see a rose and pick it, the rose is only a rose. But if the person whom you love the most gives you that rose, it becomes more. It becomes a symbol of love that is beyond the understanding of those who have not entered into such a relationship. To those who love the Lord, the act of taking Communion is one of the most significant acts in life.

The Lord's Supper is a time of remembrance. We are to remember our Lord, but in a certain way. Suppose it had been left to the apostles to design a memorial of their Master—what would they have chosen? They probably would have decided on some aspect of His ministry that had appealed to their imagination or demonstrated His popularity. They might have commissioned a plaque with some of His teachings inscribed on it, or a statue showing Him raising the dead. But Jesus did not want to be remembered first as a teacher or a miracle worker; He wanted to be remembered as the *Saviour*. That's why He chose His death for us to remember.

Through the sacrifice of Christ on Calvary, we have escaped certain death and the whiplashes of our pharaoh, Satan. We have been miraculously delivered from an eternal Egypt. We have been accepted into the family of God and are now spiritual Israel.

Can you imagine the pathos, the emotion, that must have been expressed on the faces of the Jews who escaped the slavery of Egypt? Can you imagine how frustrated they must have become when the next generation took their liberty and freedom for granted?

We are not the second, third, or fourth generation from deliverance. We have *personally* received deliverance through Christ and His death on Calvary. When we partake of the Lord's Supper, we should remember our deliverance from the guilt and power of sin with deep emotion and grateful hearts.

The Lord's Supper is a time of soul searching. "Let a man examine himself, and so let him eat of that bread, and drink of that cup" (1 Corinthians 11:28). Who are we to examine? *Ourselves,* in the light of Christ's death. We are not to examine the church, our families, or someone else. One day, we are going to stand alone before God, and we will have to answer for ourselves. We will have to stand on our own record and take personal responsibility for our faith. What terrible dread comes over us, until we remember Christ's death and how we relate to it in determining our eternal destiny.

Examine yourself. What are you trusting in? In whom are you trusting? Our good works are as filthy rags until we throw ourselves on Him. We must examine our hearts and then realize that Christ's death is the answer to our sin and weaknesses. His blood has power to remove our iniquities. One look at a brazen serpent that was lifted up for the dying, saved a nation. And one look at the Christ of the cross, and our souls are saved. Examine yourself. Are you trusting wholly in Jesus?

We are not to come to His table with pride. There is nothing we can do but to come in our need to *receive* of the Lord. We have nothing to offer. We must humble ourselves and recognize our total inability to save ourselves.

Neither are we to come to His table with dread. He has given us the invitation. His motivation is *love.* Too many people want to punish themselves, but it is only the punishment He bore that can remove the penalty of sin.

We are to come to His table with *faith.* After examining ourselves, we must focus with earnest expectation on His life, death, and victory.

The Lord's Supper is a time to anticipate our

Lord's return. He promised His disciples that He would drink with them again when the kingdom of God is fulfilled. The coming of Christ should always be in the mind of the believer. Someday, the One who has invited us to His table, time and again, will be there himself to fulfill the promise.

We are to look at the Lord's Supper from three perspectives of time: We are to remember the covenant that was sealed in the past by the death of Christ. We are to examine our faith in the present, and seek to glorify Christ through our total trust in Him. And we are to anticipate the future, which has been made certain by the work and word of Christ.

What are the emblems? The bread and the fruit of the vine. Christ said the bread is His body (Matthew 26:26). By this, however, He did not mean the bread is His *literal* body, anymore than He meant He was a literal vine when He said, "I am the vine" (John 15:5).

The bread is the symbol of His body, which was broken for our sins. He is the Bread of Life, and through His brokenness, He is able to feed the hungry souls of men. There is no other bread to sustain our souls. He is the Living Bread, the Staff of all spiritual life. There can be no substitute to meet man's hunger. He bore our sins in His body. But the punishment He took brought our *healing*. "With his stripes we are healed" (Isaiah 53:5).

Of the fruit of the vine, Jesus said, "This is my blood" (Matthew 26:28). He did not mean it was His literal blood, just as He didn't mean He was a literal light when He said, "I am the light of the world" (John 8:12). The fruit of the vine is the symbol of the blood He shed for the redemption of man's soul.

Many years ago, the United States entered into an

agreement with France, and the Louisiana Purchase was made. It was the greatest single purchase and the most important piece of property in our national history. But there was one purchase made on Calvary which makes every other purchase pale into insignificance. It was the purchase of my soul by the precious blood of the Lamb of God.

With these two ordinances of the Church we proclaim God's love to the whole world. There is no other love like it. To love an equal is human. To love one who is less fortunate is beautiful. To love one who is more fortunate is rare. But to love an enemy is divine. Through water baptism and Communion, we draw nigh to God by faith in His kindness toward us through Christ Jesus.

7

Holy Spirit Power—
Too Good to Pass Up

The Baptism in the Holy Ghost

All believers are entitled to and should ardently expect and earnestly seek the promise of the Father, the baptism in the Holy Ghost and fire, according to the command of our Lord Jesus Christ. This was the normal experience of all in the early Christian Church. With it comes the enduement of power for life and service, the bestowment of the gifts and their uses in the work of the ministry (Luke 24:49; Acts 1:4,8; 1 Corinthians 12:1-31). This experience is distinct from and subsequent to the experience of the new birth (Acts 8:12-17; 10:44-46; 11:14-16; 15:7-9). With the baptism in the Holy Ghost come such experiences as an overflowing fullness of the Spirit (John 7:37-39; Acts 4:8), a deepened reverence for God (Acts 2:43; Hebrews 12:28), an intensified consecration to God and dedication to His work (Acts 2:42), and a more active love for Christ, for His Word, and for the lost (Mark 16:20).

While the world denies our Lord Jesus and marshals a hundred arguments for not believing in His saving power, millions are meeting the living Saviour in a life-changing experience based on the written Word and the finished work of Calvary.

While many well-meaning ministers and faithful church members are denying the baptism in the Spirit in the Pentecostal sense, millions throughout the world are claiming the promise of the Father and entering a spiritual dimension in Christ that was previously unknown to them. As a result, they are receiving power for witnessing and for living the Christian life.

At the point of my need, it was enough for me to realize that God has promised the gift of eternal life through His Son Jesus. I certainly did not understand all the mechanics of salvation (and I still don't!), but I knew I needed it. When I accepted God's promised salvation, I received the gift of eternal life.

In the same manner, I learned that God the Father has given His children a promise. Before He left His disciples, Jesus told them: "And, behold, I send the promise of my Father upon you: but tarry ye in the city of Jerusalem, until ye be endued with power from on high" (Luke 24:49). The Bible assures us that our Heavenly Father knows how to give good gifts to His children: "If ye then, being evil, know how to give good gifts unto your children; how much more shall your heavenly Father give the Holy Spirit to them that ask him?" (Luke 11:13).

I wanted everything God had for me. I learned that God the Father had promised me the gift of the Holy Spirit; Jesus, the Son, had promised to send the Comforter; and the Bible promised that, in the last days, God would pour out His Spirit upon all flesh. According to the Book of Acts, the sign of speaking with other tongues at Pentecost was of God. So I decided to ask God for the baptism in the Holy Spirit.

I didn't ask my parents; I didn't ask my church; and I didn't ask my friends. I asked my Heavenly Father, in Jesus' name, to give me the baptism in the Holy Spirit with the evidence of speaking in tongues. Without anyone praying for me, and without others talking in tongues around me, I received the promise of the Father. I was filled with the Holy Spirit and spoke with other tongues as the Spirit gave me utterance.

The Baptism Is Not the New Birth

The baptism in the Holy Spirit with the evidence of speaking in tongues is distinct from and follows the new birth. Every born-again believer has the Holy Spirit dwelling in him. If a person does not have the Holy Spirit dwelling in him, he is not a true believer. We are born again by the Spirit. We are adopted and baptized by the Spirit into the body of Christ. All of these statements are Biblical statements.

When we are born again, our spirits are made alive, making spiritual life possible. Before salvation we were dead in sin, but now we are alive unto God. Our first birth in the flesh made life in and by the flesh possible. Our second birth makes life in and by the Spirit possible.

Jesus was born in the flesh by the Holy Spirit. In order to bring spiritual life to dead souls, He had to come in the flesh. But He was not contaminated or corrupted by the flesh. Even though Jesus was born of the Holy Spirit, His birth did not complete the ministry of the Holy Spirit in Him. The Bible tells us that Jesus, our Pattern, was baptized in water, and when He came up out of the water, the Spirit of God in the form of a dove came upon Him. After being led by the Spirit into the wilderness, He came out of the wilderness in the power of the Spirit.

Jesus was born or conceived by the Holy Spirit, and every believer is also born or conceived by the Holy Spirit at the time of his second birth. Jesus had the distinct experience of having the Holy Spirit come upon Him in a new and powerful way at the time of His water baptism. Christ, as our example, shows us that birth by the Holy Spirit in no way completes the gifts and ministries of the Holy Spirit in our lives. Through the second birth, we do not inherit the limitations of our parents, but the potential of our Heavenly Father.

In John 7, we read of Christ's ministry at the Feast of Tabernacles. Jesus stood and cried, "If any man thirst, let him come unto me, and drink. . . . As the Scripture hath said, out of his belly shall flow rivers of living water" (John 7:37,38). The Bible tells us He was speaking of the Spirit, "for the Holy Ghost was not yet given" (v. 39). Obviously, the Holy Spirit had been at work before the foundation of the world. So what did Jesus mean?

When people are born of the Spirit, they thirst for more of God. Why? Because anyone born of the Spirit will normally *thirst for the Spirit*. Jesus was assuring us the Holy Spirit would be given in a way He had never been given before, and in a measure the believer had never known before. He was promising an outpouring of spiritual power from within the believer that could only be compared to *rivers* of living water.

If the baptism in the Holy Spirit is not distinct from the baptism into the body of Christ, why did Jesus tell His disciples, who were certainly born again, to go and wait for the Holy Spirit to come? Why did Paul ask the Ephesians if they had received the Holy Spirit *since,* or after, they had believed

(Acts 19:2)? Why did Jesus encourage us to ask the Father for the gift of the Holy Spirit? (See Luke 11:13.)

New life by the Spirit of God makes us alive to God, but the new birth also brings a new hunger. God has promised to satisfy that hunger by the gift of the Holy Spirit, which was promised by the Father and given at Pentecost: "Repent, and be baptized every one of you in the name of Jesus Christ for the remission of sins [the new birth], and ye shall receive the gift of the Holy Ghost" (Acts 2:38). Peter assured the believers: "For the promise is unto you, and to your children [not just the apostles], and to all that are afar off" (v. 39). He made this promise to multitudes of people, not just a few, and to all believers in the future.

We believe on the basis of God's Word that the child of God may ask for and receive the gift of the Holy Spirit. This enduement of power is distinct from and subsequent to the ministry of the Holy Spirit at the time of salvation.

The Baptism Is for All Believers

Many ask if all believers are promised the baptism in the Holy Spirit with the evidence of speaking with other tongues. Let us remember what happened at Pentecost. The disciples were told to go to Jerusalem and wait for the promise of the Father. The Bible says: "They were *all* filled with the Holy Ghost" (Acts 2:4). Who were these people? They were the church. It would do no violence to the intent of Scripture to say: "And the entire church was filled with the Holy Spirit, and the entire church began to speak with other tongues."

The Bible teaches that God will give the Holy

63

Spirit to those who ask Him. Jesus said: "I send the promise of my Father" (Luke 24:49). In Joel 2:28, God says: "I will pour out my Spirit upon all flesh." At Pentecost, God did not send the Holy Spirit to just the disciples, but to the Church.

In *The Spirit Works Today,* Frank Boyd comments on Peter's sermon at Pentecost:

> The expression "to all that are afar off" was often used by Jewish rabbis to refer to the Gentiles. . . . "As many as the Lord our God shall call"—this meant that the glorious experience of the baptism in the Holy Spirit was appointed by God for every believer from the Day of Pentecost down to the end of the present age. The infilling of the Spirit, attested by the speaking with tongues as at Pentecost, was to be the pattern for that experience for every individual throughout the *Church dispensation.* (Frank M. Boyd, *The Spirit Works Today* [Springfield, MO: Gospel Publishing House, 1970], p. 71.)

The Scriptures nowhere indicate that God decided to discontinue the baptism in the Holy Spirit, or withhold His gifts when the last apostle died. On the contrary, the Bible clearly tells us there will be an acceleration of the Spirit's activity in the last days.

Those who use the phrase "whether there be tongues, they shall cease" as a proof that tongues have ceased in this generation, fail to read the next part of the verse: "Whether there be knowledge, it shall vanish away" (1 Corinthians 13:8). They use this verse to try to prove tongues have ceased, but they are not ready for one moment to try and prove that knowledge has vanished away.

The baptism in the Holy Spirit was given to the Church, and I am part of the Church. The gift of the Holy Spirit was given to all God's children because it is the promise of the Father, and I am God's child. The Holy Spirit is promised to those who ask. I asked, and I received because God keeps His promises.

Why should every believer ask for and receive the baptism in the Holy Spirit with the evidence of speaking in tongues?

The baptism in the Holy Spirit is a *promise* from God, who knows what is best for us and provides the gifts needed for His children (Acts 1:4). It is a bit surprising to see born-again Christians who are not hungering and thirsting after all God has offered to them. This promise is from our wonderful Heavenly Father, not some far-out church group or wild-eyed prophet.

The devil must be delighted when he sees a believer held back from God's wonderful blessing because of some misunderstanding. Can you imagine how it must grieve God when His children do not ask for and receive His gift? Imagine if your father excitedly promised you a very special gift, but then you never seemed to care enough to ask him for it!

How God must be grieved by His children's fear concerning the baptism in the Holy Spirit! Some of God's children are so filled with fear that they actually believe if they ask their Heavenly Father for the infilling of the Holy Spirit, they might receive something from the devil.

Let me promise you, the devil is delighted by this terrible misconception. The whole dimension of fear surrounding spiritual gifts is of the devil and is completely contrary to Scripture. The Bible says God loves us. The Bible says if we ask our Father for bread, He will not give us a stone, or if we ask for a

65

fish, He will not give us a serpent. It is almost blasphemous to even suggest that a person who honestly claims a Biblical promise, a promise from God, is in any danger from the devil. The fact that there is a spiritual battle is simply proof we are making the enemy angry—not that we are on the enemy's side.

We must not let some well-intentioned preacher keep us from claiming, asking for, and receiving our Heavenly Father's gifts. Our Father has promised us the baptism in the Holy Spirit. No authority on earth can keep us from receiving the promise of our Father, and we should not allow anyone to keep us from receiving all God has promised us.

Results of Receiving the Baptism

The baptism in the Holy Spirit is *power* from God. The *dunamis,* or dynamite, of God is made available through the Church and to the Church. The Holy Spirit anointed Jesus of Nazareth and gave Him power or authority over every power or authority that would stand in the way of God's glory on earth.

The Scriptures are clear. We are in a spiritual conflict; we wrestle against principalities and powers. The enemy has come in like a flood. Let us not be mistaken, Satan has growing power in this world. More and more vehicles for demonic activity are being made available to the forces of evil. The church of Jesus Christ needs to take power and authority over the devil, but none of us is naive enough to believe the devil is afraid of the Church in and by itself. The Church must ask for and receive the power of the Holy Spirit in order to destroy Satan's kingdom.

But what is the Church? It is the spiritual

building of God consisting of living stones. Every believer, made part of the true Church through faith, has a responsibility to claim the promise of the Father and receive spiritual power from God. That special enduement of power from on high is promised to the believer when he receives the gift of the Holy Spirit.

The baptism in the Holy Spirit brings *glory* to God. Jesus said we would have power to be witnesses for Christ after the Spirit comes upon us.

The ultimate purpose for seeking the fullness of the Spirit is to be a witness for Christ in every part of life; to be so identified with the living Lord that He can be seen in us by everyone with whom we come in contact.

The Baptism will enhance our witness for Christ through our *lives*. People will come to know Jesus through us. The Baptism helps make Christ so real to the believer that Jesus will become everything. In speaking of the disciples, the Bible says the officials "took note that these men had been with Jesus" (Acts 4:13, NIV). Out of our innermost being will flow rivers of living water—a power source in a world where spiritual power has failed. The Spirit-empowered life will be a supernatural life and will bring glory to Jesus.

The Baptism will enhance our witness for Christ through our *words*. The Word of God had to become flesh to have any real witness. In the same sense, our words are powerless in themselves, but when we are full of God's power, we will speak the words of life with revelation and power. No man can really say, "Jesus is Lord," except by the Holy Spirit. It is hard to fully realize how important it is to be full of the Holy Spirit when we speak about Jesus.

The Baptism will also enhance our witness for Christ through our *works*. There has never been a time when the need was greater for the supernatural power of the Spirit to work in and through the Body. When Jesus was alive on this earth, His works brought glory to God. Mighty things were done through Jesus by the Spirit's power. Jesus is no longer with us in the flesh, but His body, the Church, is here, and we are part of that Body.

If Christ was anointed by the Spirit to witness of the Father, how much more must we, as His body, be anointed to be witnesses of Christ, so men may come to know God and glorify Him on earth.

8

Tongues—Real or Counterfeit?

The Evidence of the Baptism in the Holy Ghost

The baptism of believers in the Holy Ghost is witnessed by the initial physical sign of speaking with other tongues as the Spirit of God gives them utterance (Acts 2:4). The speaking in tongues in this instance is the same in essence as the gift of tongues (1 Corinthians 12:4-10,28), but different in purpose and use.

At the turn of this century, a group of students in Topeka, Kansas, were studying about the person and ministry of the Holy Spirit. They read about the promise of the Father, they understood from the Scriptures that Jesus had promised the Holy Spirit to those who asked, and they further learned that the promise of the Holy Spirit was to all generations.

Through their leader, Charles Parham, God placed within their hearts a divine curiosity to determine what evidence, if any, a person could have to confirm that he had received the gift of the Holy Ghost. How could a person prove to himself, the church, and/or the devil, that he had indeed received the baptism in the Holy Spirit? As was their custom, the students studied independently for a period of time, using the Bible as their textbook.

After earnest study, they reassembled to make their report. To their amazement, they had all come to the same conclusion: the evidence a person would receive when he or she received the baptism in the Holy Spirit would be speaking in an unknown tongue.

On the first day of 1901, Agnes Ozman became the first student in the group to ask in faith and receive the baptism in the Holy Spirit with the evidence of speaking in other tongues. Soon thousands of people throughout the United States and around the world were awakened to this great Biblical truth and received the infilling of the Holy Spirit.

It is not difficult to imagine the effect such an awakening had on the established church. A formidable line of defense was drawn against this Holy Spirit renewal. People who testified to receiving the Baptism with the evidence of speaking in tongues were put out of their churches. Preachers who opened their hearts to receive the infilling were expelled from their denominations as heretics.

So many preachers and church members were made religious outcasts that the inevitable happened. In the year 1914, a large group of Spirit-baptized believers met in Hot Springs, Arkansas, and the Assemblies of God was formed as a cooperative fellowship.

In less than 100 years, this Pentecostal movement has swept the globe. In spite of persecution, excesses, and spiritual warfare, the Scriptures are being literally fulfilled by the outpouring of the Holy Spirit with the physical evidence of speaking in other tongues.

Our Distinctive Reason for Being

The doctrinal position of the Assemblies of God concerning speaking in tongues makes our movement distinct from other evangelical and fundamentalist churches. The basic reason we are in the body of Christ is because of the person and ministry of Christ. The Assemblies of God's distinctive reason for being is our teaching on the evidence of the Baptism.

Anyone who has received Jesus Christ and been born again of the Spirit has been baptized by the Spirit into the body of Christ. The Assemblies of God teaches that speaking in other tongues is not part of the doctrine of salvation. To put it plainly, we believe it is not necessary to receive the gift of the Holy Spirit in order to receive the gift of eternal life. However, all believers who are members of the Assemblies of God as a cooperative fellowship, state by their membership that they believe in speaking with other tongues as *the* evidence, not *an* evidence, of the baptism in the Holy Spirit.

God has placed in His body distinctive individual and corporate entities. We are all one in Christ, but we are different from other members of the body of Christ. However, the Bible is clear in assuring us that differences are not a threat to the body of Christ, and furthermore, the unity of distinctive parts fitly framed together is a powerful testimony to the world.

Our country is a perfect example; one of the mottoes of the United States is *e pluribus unum.* We are 50 states, but we come under one federal head. In the same way, the body of Christ is a perfect union of member churches in the Body, under the federal Head of the universal Church, Jesus Christ.

71

An inadequate, but helpful illustration would be to imagine the body of Christ as a united kingdom, and the different church bodies as states within the united kingdom. In the "United Kingdom of God" we have the Methodist state, the Presbyterian state, the Nazarene state, the Foursquare state, the Assemblies of God state, etc. Each state within the U.S. has unique and different qualifications and responsibilities.

When I became an American citizen, I was legally born again on this earth. My old country "passed away," and behold, all things became new because I lived and moved in a new land. For a while, I chose to live in a state in the East. Then I progressed to a state in the Midwest, and finally I came into a new dimension of fullness by moving to the state of California. While I lived in each state I was still an American. But when I moved to California, I also became a Californian by accepting its distinct rules, regulations, and benefits.

In Jesus Christ, I was translated out of the kingdom of darkness into the kingdom of light. However, in the kingdom of God, I settled into the Assemblies of God state because I believed it had special blessings and benefits according to the divine constitution. It is silly for us to let our differences under Christ separate us, just as it is silly for state boundaries to separate Californians from Oregonians. We are one in the bonds of the United States, but we respect each other under our different state charters.

My claim to freedom from the domination of other countries is the fact that my citizenship is in Washington, D.C. However, I choose to work and reside in California, so in addition to my responsibilities as an American citizen, I have responsibilities as a California resident.

In Jesus Christ, my spiritual citizenship is in heaven, but as long as the body of Christ is on earth, I have to choose a religious state or denomination through which to serve God.

In 1914, the spiritual state of the Assemblies of God was founded. Every born-again believer may join the Assemblies of God, but first he must recognize that we ask that all members believe that speaking in tongues is the initial physical evidence of the baptism in the Holy Spirit. By definition, all Assemblies of God members believe this distinction. To say I am a member of the Assemblies of God, and at the same time say I don't believe speaking in tongues is the physical evidence of the Baptism, would be like saying I am a resident of California, but I don't believe a person has to pay state income taxes as a California resident. By definition, a Californian believes he had better pay taxes!

I have used a negative illustration to make my point, but in the positive sense, all those who belong to the Assemblies of God are saying by their action that they believe in this tenet of faith.

The Initial Physical Evidence

Why do residents in the state of the Assemblies of God believe that speaking in tongues is *the* initial physical evidence of the baptism in the Holy Spirit?

We believe there is a *scriptural pattern* for speaking in tongues as the initial physical evidence of the Baptism. Nowhere does the Bible state that the physical evidence of the Baptism is speaking in other tongues. But neither does it say there are three Persons in the Godhead; nor does it mention the word *Trinity*. But all evangelical teachers believe the Trinity is a Biblical doctrine.

We believe that a Biblical principle, linked with a Biblical pattern, is a Biblical doctrine. The Baptism, with the initial physical evidence of speaking in other tongues, is a Biblical principle. The fountainhead of our teaching is from the Word of God.

Biblical prophecy foretold the Baptism. Isaiah said: "For with stammering lips and another tongue will he speak to this people" (Isaiah 28:11). The prophet Joel foretold the principle of the Spirit's outpouring (Joel 2:28,29).

Jesus Christ himself promised it in the Father's name: "It is expedient for you that I go away: for if I go not away, the Comforter will not come unto you; but if I depart, I will send him unto you" (John 16:7). "I send the promise of my Father upon you" (Luke 24:49). "Ye shall receive power, after that the Holy Ghost is come upon you" (Acts 1:8). Jesus established the principle and commanded the disciples to go to Jerusalem and wait until they received the power of God through the outpouring of the Holy Spirit.

The Day of Pentecost fulfilled the principle and established the pattern of evidence. Things happened to the believers at Pentecost. There was "a sound from heaven as of a rushing mighty wind," and "tongues like as of fire" sat upon them (Acts 2:1-3). But what happened *in* and *through* them was the evidence of the Baptism: "And they were all filled with the Holy Ghost, and began to *speak with other tongues,* as the Spirit gave them utterance" (Acts 2:4).

This Biblical pattern was established as the initial physical proof of the Baptism. In Acts 10, the pattern was continued. The only way the Jews knew the Holy Spirit had fallen on the Gentiles was by a physical sign: "For they heard them *speak with tongues*" (Acts 10:46). In Acts 19, we discover that the same thing happened in Ephesus.

Throughout the New Testament God inspired men to share the principle of the Baptism. He did not always choose to share the pattern over and over in detail, but wherever He did, the pattern was consistent—they spoke in other tongues.

The Church continued the Biblical doctrine of the Baptism. The New Testament Church and the Early Church fathers spoke often of the Baptism. History records that the Biblical pattern continued.

We believe the Baptism is *dispensational* in emphasis. Many people doubt the validity of the Baptism because they have not seen the same emphasis on it throughout the Church Age. Yet, these same people do not deny the doctrine of justification by faith just because the Church did not teach and emphasize it for centuries. But one day, Martin Luther had a revelation of Biblical truth that became the doctrine God used to revive and revolutionize the Church.

The fullness of the Spirit has dispensational overtones. Joel's prophecy clearly indicates that it is in the last days that God has promised His people the former and latter rain. Just as Luther received the revelation of the neglected doctrine of justification by faith, so at the turn of the century people who were seeking God received the revelation of the Baptism. It was not a new revelation, but a neglected Biblical principle and pattern. Throughout Church history believers have received the Baptism, but now, just before the end of the age,

God is fulfilling His promise to pour out His Spirit upon all flesh. Knowing that Satan is coming against the bride of Christ with fresh zeal, God is preparing a victorious and overcoming Church for the Rapture.

We believe the Baptism is an individual experience. Although our church fellowship believes and preaches the Baptism, the Assemblies of God is not a building or denomination. Rather, it is the communion of individually born-again believers who have asked for and received the baptism in the Holy Spirit.

God gives the Baptism to those who ask. The baptism in the Holy Spirit is given to the individual to enable him to win his world for Jesus Christ. No age, church, or authority can block the child of God from receiving the Baptism. It is a specific promise from God to His children; He *will* give the Holy Spirit to those who ask.

The Purpose of Speaking in Tongues

We believe the initial physical evidence of speaking in tongues differs in purpose from the gift of tongues. The evidence of speaking in tongues is the proof or sign of the Baptism. The gift of tongues is a ministry of the Holy Spirit.

The distinction between the initial gift of the Holy Spirit himself, with the evidence of tongues, and the subsequent gift of "kinds of tongues," is very carefully preserved in the New Testament. The Greek word used in the New Testament for the gift of the Holy Spirit received at the baptism in the Spirit is always the word *dorea*. The Greek word *charisma* (translated "gift") is used to denote any of the nine gifts or manifestations (including the gift of

76

tongues). There is a clear distinction between these two aspects of spiritual experience.

All who receive the baptism in the Holy Spirit speak with other tongues, but all do not receive the *gift* of tongues. The evidence of tongues and the gift of tongues differ in their purpose, although they are the same in essence. This is the reason people come to wrong conclusions when they try to encompass speaking in tongues in one purpose.

Speaking in tongues is the initial physical evidence of something greater than tongues—the baptism in the Holy Spirit.

Some people may ask, "Why do you need the Baptism?" The fullness of the Spirit opens up channels of blessing for power and witnessing because the Spirit is given to *glorify* Jesus. When a person is born again, he is made alive spiritually. To have the gift of the Holy Spirit is to have the potential of a life completely controlled and guided by the Spirit. The Baptism identifies the believer with the life of the Spirit. The Baptism opens up doors of potentiality in God, and it is the Father's promise to His children.

Some may question, "Why did God choose tongues as the evidence of the Baptism?" The Bible does not tell us directly, but we offer the following reasons.

1. Matthew 12:34 says: "Out of the abundance of the heart the mouth speaketh." Obviously, if the inner man is totally submerged in the supernatural flow of the Holy Spirit, the mouth will produce supernatural expressions from that same Holy Spirit. The Holy Spirit is a Person who desires to express himself through the communication provided by the human tongue.

77

2. The tongue is the universal means of communicating. How wise for the universal Spirit to use this means of expression to tell the believer and the world that the Holy Spirit has filled the individual.

3. According to the Book of James, the tongue cannot be tamed by man (James 3:8). When a person speaks with supernatural tongues, that person is under the influence of the Holy Spirit, and even the most unruly member of the body is guided by the Spirit.

4. Speaking with tongues makes the Baptism a conscious experience; it is a physical evidence that the devil has difficulty denying. Can you imagine how effective Satan would be in throwing doubt on this experience if there were no physical evidence?

The Gift of Tongues

The Baptism opens up for the believer the possibility of receiving the *gift of tongues*. Let us divide the ministry of the gift of tongues into two basic areas: tongues as a prayer language, and tongues as individual edification.

The reason we need the gift of tongues is to have power with God in *prayer*. In this context, the Bible says: "He that speaketh in an unknown tongue speaketh not unto men, but unto God: for no man understandeth him; howbeit in the spirit he speaketh mysteries" (1 Corinthians 14:2). It is a blow to our pride to accept the Bible's declaration that we lack knowledge in praying, but the Spirit himself will make intercession for us with groanings which cannot be uttered (Romans 8:26). And the Spirit always intercedes for us in accordance with God's will (Romans 8:27).

The gift of tongues also serves as a blessing from God to *edify* the individual believer: "He that speaketh in an unknown tongue edifieth himself" (1 Corinthians 14:4). Paul found the ministry of tongues so edifying that he said, "I thank my God, I speak with tongues more than ye all" (1 Corinthians 14:18). Personally, I can attest to this in my own busy life as a pastor. Time and again in my private devotions, I have enjoyed being edified in my soul through the ministry of tongues.

The gift of tongues is also a spiritual gift to edify the Church. It was in this context that Paul wrote to the church at Corinth. They had misunderstood, or were deliberately misusing, the gift. In chapters 12 and 14 of 1 Corinthians, Paul carefully outlines the use of the gift of tongues. If a person speaks in tongues in public, he is to pray for an interpretation to be given (1 Corinthians 14:13).

In the case of public worship, it is considered especially beneficial to prophesy, because prophecy is given in the language known to the people. Thus, the exhortation is given to insist on interpretation following speaking in tongues. In the congregation, there should be no more than two or three manifestations of tongues with their interpretation, and they should be given in an orderly and proper manner. Also, the congregation is responsible for judging the contents of the message to assure the validity of the gift and to maintain Biblical doctrine.

If we have all these regulations, why are tongues and interpretation needed in a congregation? Tongues and interpretation are one of God's ways of edifying the Church and making people more God-conscious. Also, God has given many safeguards, and He has assured us that He gives His gifts to the

Church as He desires. God has given spiritual leadership for direction and instruction in the manifestation of spiritual gifts.

Tongues are also given as a *sign* to the unbeliever. Throughout history, there have been people who were dramatically brought to a saving knowledge of Christ through hearing a Spirit-filled believer speak in what was an unknown tongue to that believer, but the native tongue of the sinner.

God's gifts are given to help us spiritually. It is understood that the Baptism is not the proof of the Spirit-filled life, because the fruit of the Spirit fulfills that role. But there are no honest Christians who would readily deny that they need all the help they can get to live a spiritually powerful, overcoming life.

The promise of the Father is yours. He will give the Holy Spirit to those who ask. Don't settle for anything less than the Biblical principle—the baptism in the Holy Spirit—and the Biblical pattern—receiving the Baptism with the evidence of speaking in other tongues.

How can you receive the Baptism? Recognize your place in Christ. If your sins have been forgiven, you are a child of God. You are in a position to claim the promise of the Father because you are His child.

Ask for the Baptism in Jesus' name. He has promised to give the Holy Spirit to those who ask Him.

Take a step of faith like Peter did when he stepped out of the boat. Begin to praise God, and remember, He promises to give you the utterance.

9

Christians—In Spite of Everything

Sanctification

Sanctification is an act of separation from that which is evil, and of dedication unto God (Romans 12:1,2; 1 Thessalonians 5:23; Hebrews 13:12). The Scriptures teach a life of "holiness without which no man shall see the Lord" (Hebrews 12:14). By the power of the Holy Ghost we are able to obey the command: "Be ye holy, for I am holy" (1 Peter 1:15,16).

Sanctification is realized in the believer by recognizing his identification with Christ in His death and resurrection, and by faith reckoning daily upon the fact of that union, and by offering every faculty continually to the dominion of the Holy Spirit (Romans 6:1-11,13; 8:1,2,13; Galatians 2:20; Philippians 2:12,13; 1 Peter 1:5).

Our statement of faith regarding sanctification is in itself a beautiful definition of this misunderstood and mistreated subject.

In Genesis 2:3 we are told that God blessed the Sabbath Day and sanctified it. Two things about this divine act will help us grasp the power and meaning behind the sanctified life.

First, God blessed the Sabbath Day by *setting it apart* from other days. It was to be a day of holiness and blessing. In the same way, the Christian is to be

81

set apart from the world; reserved for God's glory, use, and purpose. But this is intended to be a *blessing* and a *privilege*, not a dreaded duty.

Second, the institution of the Sabbath Day must have brought a glorious response from the hosts of heaven. The setting aside of a day for God is most admirable, but the power of the Sabbath is not in its being established, but in its being consistently used to *glorify God.*

The sanctified or holy life must be seen in the same way. God declares us righteous or sanctified at the moment of salvation. We are set free from the law of sin and death. One minute we are defiled, guilty sinners facing the judgment of God's wrath, and the next moment we are declared clean of all sin—just as if we had never sinned. The power of the sanctified life, however, is not limited to the declaration of our position in God; it is in demonstrated progress in that new position.

Positional Sanctification

As a sinner, we begin to put our faith in Jesus Christ. God, in turn, has a great deal of faith in us. We become (positionally) new creatures. We are born again and adopted into the family of God. Our Lord now expects us to use our position in Him to live an overcoming life—a life of love and service.

We can illustrate this by the following. Suppose a married couple have a great deal of trouble because the husband is a scoundrel, a thief, and a wife beater. Under the law, the wife is married to the man. But one day the husband drops dead. At that moment, the wife is free to marry someone else. She falls in love with another man and marries him. The moment they are pronounced man and wife, the woman is married to another husband. Her position in life has changed. The old life is dead; the former husband has no power over her. She is now married to another.

However, being declared married only makes married life possible. The bride has not only claimed the position of marriage, but also assumed the responsibility of marriage. She may choose to be faithful, putting her whole being into the marriage, or she may fall into the trap of listening to others. "Marriages are failing," trumpet the headlines. "Open marriages are condoned," says a leading marriage authority. "Adultery can be helpful," writes a magazine columnist. The bride has a choice to make. Will she honor her commitment to God and her husband? Will she keep herself for him alone? Will she use her position to bless the union, or will she try to be married only part of the time?

The picture of marriage helps us to visualize what sanctification means. The Bible tells us that under the Law we were bound to sin and death. But through Jesus Christ, we are set free from the law of sin and death. We reckon ourselves, in Christ, as dead; we are divorced from the guilt and authority of sin. By a divine act of love, we are placed into the body of Christ. At that moment we become His; we are His bride. This is the *initial act of separation.* We tell the whole world we are set apart; we are sanctified to Christ.

At salvation we are declared sanctified, and after salvation we must decide whether or not to live the sanctified life. We must choose to be faithful to our Lord, or faithless. We must choose to live to please God, or self. We must choose to obey Jesus, or obey the world.

All of this leads to the central truth of sanctification. We are held personally responsible for our relationship with God in the same way that a married couple is held responsible for being faithful and building a life together. There is a position to be honored and progress to be made.

There are those who teach that sanctification is an experience like the baptism in the Holy Spirit. They call it the "second definite work of grace." They teach the death of the "old man," or that he needs to be put to death, so they seek an experience of sanctification. When they receive this experience, the old man is declared dead, so they are not bothered by him anymore.

We believe an experience of sanctification is received at salvation; it is the sanctification wrought by Christ. We believe that from that moment we have the authority to reckon ourselves dead to the old life, but there is still a constant spiritual warfare. Christians may not seek sin, but sin seeks Christians. So we must choose each day to follow the Lord. Paul said, "I die daily" (1 Corinthians 15:31). The ego, the self, needs to be put to death. At salvation we are brought into a position of righteousness, but we must daily die to self and strive to be conformed to the image of the Son. This needs to be said clearly to every believer. God is going to hold us personally responsible for moral sensitivity and excellence.

Progressive Sanctification

Too many are pointing to the world and blaming the world system for their own lack of moral commitment. The world is wicked. The Bible tells us we are living in a crooked and perverse generation.

But we are no longer *of* the world, even though we are *in* the world. We are free from the authority of the worldly spirit. Our kingdom is not of this world. The scepter of the world's kingdom may be anti-Christ, but the scepter of God's kingdom is the righteousness of Christ himself.

Too many are excusing themselves from moral responsibility and holiness because they are weak in the flesh. Carefully examine those who do not choose to overcome and who actually allow themselves to constantly fall into sin. Over a long period of time, you will discover that any person who excuses himself from holy living because of his own inadequacies is not allowing Christ to live *through* him. According to Scripture, anyone who wants to be filled with the righteousness of Christ may be. All one needs is a hunger for righteousness. The Bible further tells us:

> Do not offer the parts of your body to sin, as instruments of wickedness, but rather offer yourselves to God, as those who have been brought from death to life; and offer the parts of your body to him as instruments of righteousness (Romans 6:13, NIV).

To those who say, "I can't live the life," we must insist that they are really saying, "I *choose* not to live the life"—for we have this promise: "I can do all things through Christ which strengtheneth me" (Philippians 4:13).

There are two fatal flaws in those who blame their weakness for their not living a godly life. First, there is a lack of desire to live a life of holiness. There is more *excusing* of sin than *repentance* of sin. Second, there is a lack of striving or *discipline* in holy living. There is a greater desire for comfort than for conviction; there is more compromise than war against evil in their life.

Too many are pointing to the church and blaming it for their lack of dedicated righteousness to God. But who is the church? The church is made up of individuals—it is me; it is you. Christ died to save the individual in the church. Christ lives to justify the believer in the church. The Holy Spirit comes to empower the saint in the church.

Notice the thrust of the Spirit's message to the churches in the Book of Revelation. In nearly every case, the church is condemned for allowing sin or false doctrine. Yet the message is clear: the Lord is telling the individual that the failures of the church are not an excuse for him to fail God. Rather, they are opportunities to live an overcoming life. The sins and failures around us should not deter us, but make us more determined.

Positive Aspects of Sanctification

We have discussed positional sanctification and personal progressive sanctification. Now we will consider the positive aspects of sanctification. The key to the whole doctrine of sanctification is being dead to sin and alive to God. Many people have become frustrated in trying to live an overcoming life because they have been trained in only one part of holiness: death to sin. But death to sin is not much good if there is no new life.

I can remember my total frustration in hearing sermon after sermon on how terrible my sins were. I would deplore my sins, surrender them all, and mutter under my breath, "I'm dead to sin. My sins are forgiven; they are under the Blood, and I'm going to heaven."

Now what? My sins are gone, the old life is gone, and the devil is gone. But I'm still here!

I was told to "live the life." "What life?" I naively asked. "The overcoming life," they would answer. (I had the distinct feeling that they wanted to add "stupid"!) "What's that?" I asked. "Overcoming the world, the flesh, and the devil," they would answer.

I didn't dare tell them what I thought. How do you overcome something that has already been overcome by the finished work of Christ on the cross?

Jesus Christ overcame the world, the flesh, and the devil. In Him, we have overcome. But a conqueror needs to do more than kill his enemies and conquer the world, he must replace what he has conquered with something better.

We are not only dead to sin, but also *alive to God.* The old life is dead, and we are alive to God as new creatures. We have new life; old things are passed away. We are called according to His purpose.

Repentance is the act of turning around and going in another direction. Sanctification is the enabling of the Lord to walk in a new direction. Progressive sanctification is exercising our will to use the imputed righteousness of Christ to be and do what He wants us to be and do. God's purpose is for our lives to bring glory to Him. Instead of living for self, we must die to self and live for Him.

What a wonderful day when World War II came to an end; everything changed. What happened? Our national purpose turned from destroying to building; from war to peace. Factories that had been turned into war-making machines began to manufacture cars. Before Christ, we manufactured those things that brought destruction. We manufactured hate, greed, bitterness, and other products born of sin. But now, in Christ, we are living for another purpose. We are called to destroy sin. But more than defeating sin and Satan, we have been set aside to bring His life into our world. Now we manufacture His love, joy, peace, and long-suffering—the fruit of the Spirit—to build up His kingdom.

Not only does sanctification give us a new purpose, it also gives us a new *power*. No longer do we live, but Christ lives in us daily. No longer do we fight evil with evil, or carnality with carnal weapons. Instead, we overcome evil with good. We replace the old life with a new life in Christ. We don't have to let sin reign in our bodies anymore, because "greater is he that is in [us], than he that is in the world" (1 John 4:4). We don't have to put up with sin in our lives any longer. Instead, we can have faith in God. He is alive and ruling in our hearts now. "We can through Christ" becomes the motto of our new life.

What do we do with the bad in our lives? We overcome by replacing it with good. Since there is none good but God, we let God rule our lives. And with God, all things are possible. Sin doesn't have power over us anymore!

Canon Aitken tells of the time he preached about overcoming evil and not letting sin reign. A young man stopped him on the way out of church to disagree with his sermon. "We don't stop sinning overnight," the young man insisted. "Christ gradually overcomes the evil. It is impossible to be perfect."

Canon Aitken smiled in response. "Young man,"

he said, "we decide daily to die to sin—that is immediate. But we are growing daily in our lives to God." Then he gave this illustration: When a pickpocket is saved, do we expect him to get up in a testimony service and say, "I used to pick 20 pockets a day. I want to praise God that I'm down now to only picking five pockets a day"? (This illustration was taken from *Keswick's Triumphant Voice,* edited by Herbert Stevenson [London: Marshall, Morgan and Scott, Ltd., 1963], p. 163.)

The apostle Paul writes: "Reckon ye also yourselves to be dead indeed unto sin, but alive unto God" (Romans 6:11). *This is your power.*

It is important for the Christian to realize that sanctification or holiness is a practical everyday process. Too many Christians feel the life of sanctification is for some "super saint" who never confronts life in a normal sense.

We can often better determine what something *is* by defining what it is *not.* Practical holiness is not innocence or ignorance of sin. Adam and Eve were the only human beings to live within the framework of innocency. Practical holiness is not the removal of the body from a sinful environment. Jesus did not pray for the removal of the believer from the world, but for the spiritual protection of the believer *in* the world. Practical holiness is not the mastery of a list of dos and don'ts. It is possible to abstain from everything labeled worldly and yet remain worldly. Worldliness is not an act, but the motivation of the heart behind the act.

Practical holiness or sanctification is *wholesomeness.* It is a wholesome attitude toward God. Worldliness is not really denying God but forgetting and ignoring Him in our decisionmaking and our everyday existence. Holiness is being God-conscious and God-honoring in a positive and wholesome obedience to the divine will.

Sanctification means having a wholesome attitude toward oneself by seeking to be spiritually edified and strong. It is an honest respect for oneself under the lordship of Christ. It also means a wholesome relationship toward everyone and everything—wholesome in appearance toward others, in conversation and communication, in life-style and family life, in money matters, and in discipline and temperament.

The world is moving further away from wholesome living, but the Christian can take heart in the fact that "greater is he that is in you, than he that is in the world" (1 John 4:4). Living a godly life in this evil world is not a terrible duty, but a wonderful privilege.

Sanctification also brings a *new potential*—perfection. Jesus said: "Be ye therefore perfect, even as your Father which is in heaven is perfect" (Matthew 5:48). Because of a new purpose and a new power, we can look ahead to God's potential in us. His perfection is possible to attain, or He would not have commanded it of us. Our Father is perfect as only God can be perfect. He commands us to be perfect as only God's children can be perfect *through His enabling grace.*

We have been sanctified by the work of Christ on Calvary. We are being sanctified as we allow God's will to be done through us. We shall be eternally and wholly sanctified when He comes again. "We shall be like him; for we shall see him as he is" (1 John 3:2).

10

The Church Is Alive and Well on Planet Earth

The Church and Its Mission

The Church is the body of Christ, the habitation of God through the Spirit, with divine appointments for the fulfillment of her great commission. Each believer, born of the Spirit, is an integral part of the General Assembly and Church of the First-born, which are written in heaven (Ephesians 1:22,23; 2:22; Hebrews 12:23). . . .

The priority reason-for-being of the Assemblies of God as a part of the Church is: (a)To be an agency of God for evangelizing the world (Acts 1:8; Matthew 28:19,20; Mark 16:15,16). (b)To be a corporate body in which man may worship God (1 Corinthians 12:13). (c)To be a channel of God's purpose to build a body of saints being perfected in the image of His Son (Ephesians 4:11-16; 1 Corinthians 12:28; 1 Corinthians 14:12).

The Assemblies of God exists expressly to give continuing emphasis to this reason-for-being in the New Testament apostolic pattern by teaching and encouraging believers to be baptized in the Holy Spirit.

There is real difficulty in defining the Church because it is both spiritual in substance and physical in expression. So first, we will determine what the Church is not. The Church is not a building; it meets *in* a building. One of the most important moments on earth is when the congregation leaves the church building and walks out to *be* the Church.

The Church is not a denomination, and it does not draw its life and authority from any man-made organization. No denomination, whether small or large, can claim to be *the* Church, because the Church is built of spiritual substance and not human design.

The Church is not an improvement on Judaism. Jesus said that He would build His church (Matthew 16:18)—something future. Judaism was simply used as a channel to help bring the Church into being.

The Church is not the kingdom of God or the kingdom of heaven. The Kingdom is much broader in scope than the Church. The Kingdom encompasses the saved of all the ages prior to Christ's coming and includes those yet unborn in the Millennium.

To better understand the meaning of the Church, we will consider some of the word pictures the Bible uses to describe the Church.

The Church as a Building

The Bible depicts the Church as a spiritual building. Usually when we think of a building we visualize an established physical structure. But we must enlarge the concept to include the building that is in the process of being built and not just the finished product.

Let us imagine a great cathedral that has taken over 200 years to build. In several historical cases, a congregation actually worshiped in such a cathedral for well over a century while the building program was completed. Jesus Christ has been building His spiritual church, "a habitation of God through the Spirit," for 2,000 years. (Ephesians 2:20-22 and 1 Peter 2:5 help to clarify this concept.)

The Church as a spiritual building has three basic facets. The first is the *foundation*. The foundation consists of Jesus Christ, who is called the Chief Cornerstone, along with the apostles and prophets. He is the stone the builders rejected. The Bible says: "He came unto his own, and his own received him not" (John 1:11). The builders (meaning, the religious tradesmen, the clergy and the priesthood) looked at the Nazarene and rejected Him as building material.

Nathanael asked, "Can there any good thing come out of Nazareth?" (John 1:46). No, nothing good can come out of Nazareth, but something wonderful came out of heaven. Romans 9:33 says: "Behold, I am laying in Zion a stone that will make men stumble, a rock that will make them fall; and he who believes in him will not be put to shame" (RSV). In a practical sense, anyone who chooses to reject Jesus, rejects the entire concept of the true Church.

The Church is built on the foundation of the apostles and prophets. Through them came the foundational truths the Bible identifies as the "faith which was once delivered unto the saints" (Jude 3). Remember, the worlds were formed by the Word of God, and so was the Church. A fundamental truth of the Church is that the Word became flesh. Jesus is the eternal, solid Rock which is unshakable and unmovable. The foundational truths of the Church are inherent in the faith that was given to the apostles and prophets as they were moved upon by the Holy Spirit.

In the eyes of God, the most important part of a

building is the foundation. In His great parable of the wise and foolish builders, Jesus carefully pointed out that wisdom concentrates on the *foundation* (Luke 6:47-49). The superstructure may vary in size and quality, but that which remains is the foundation. If the most beautiful building on earth is not built on a proper foundation, that building will collapse when the storm comes.

First Corinthians 3:11 says: "For other foundation can no man lay than that is laid, which is Jesus Christ." Paul exhorts us to build all our hopes, dreams, and visions on Christ—to make Christ central.

We must recognize that the "faith which was once delivered unto the saints" was the knowledge of Christ and His works; all other ground is sinking sand. The true Church is built on the Rock, and the gates of hell will not prevail against it. Every other religion, every other group, and every other religious organization will fail and fall when the gates of hell decide to prevail. This is why the idea of church bodies uniting in an ecumenical movement, apart from the foundational truths of Scripture, is doomed to failure. The foundation or reason for being of the true Church is not to unite all visible churches on earth, but to declare that Jesus Christ—the Word made flesh, revealed through apostolic faith—is the only ground for the Church's existence.

If someone says that Jesus Christ is the virgin-born Son of God, as revealed in the Scriptures; the Saviour of the world through His precious blood; the anointed Christ, as declared by the apostles; and our coming King—then that person is our fellow worker, and we are workers together with God. But if an angel from heaven, or a delegate from any earthly organization, tells us that he is building on a new foundation, that he has found another Jesus by the authority of God's Word, or that God has given him another faith, then we cannot bless his efforts. Rather, we must declare that he is under a curse for preaching any other gospel and building on any other foundation (Galatians 1:8,9).

The true Church is building on a foundation that will stand the test. Away with fair-weather religion! We are facing the world's greatest storms. Away with a religion of the head; we need a religion of the Rock! Who is going to stand? Those who have been more concerned about what God says rather than what men think.

Jesus is using special building materials to build His church. First Peter 2:5,9 says:

> And now you have become living building-stones for God's use in building his house. . . . You are holy and pure, you are God's very own—all this so that you may show to others how God called you out of the darkness into his wonderful light (*The Living Bible*).

Out of this world, Jesus Christ is drawing the living materials for a spiritual building—people who are alive to God. Through Him, the building is being "fitly framed together . . . unto a holy temple" (Ephesians 2:21). He *will* build His church. He has declared it.

Notice that Jesus did not say, "I will build *your* church." Many have become confused on this important point. Too many churches and denominations are trying to make Jesus fit into their ideas of doing things. Throughout the centuries, men have limited the Holy One of Israel. Jesus said, "I will build *my* church," but the Jews wanted Him to build theirs. So outside the walls of Judaism, in an upper room, 120 ordinary people gathered in obedience. Suddenly, they heard a sound from heaven as of a rushing, mighty wind. Jesus was fulfilling His promise: "I will build my church."

If we ever reach the point where our church is not His church, He will write "Ichabod" (meaning, "There is no glory") over the door of our sanctuary. And instead, He will find some little, humble "hole in the wall" in which to pour out His Spirit to reaffirm, "I will build my church"—because there is no other church to build.

Notice He did not say, "*You* will build my church." A lot of good, sincere people are trying to do by the flesh what can only be done by the Spirit of God. It is an impossible job to build the church of Jesus Christ. I am not, however, preaching a lack of involvement and discipline. On the contrary, I am preaching a greater ministry and a more effective building of the Kingdom because He promised to build His church through us. We have become living stones through the mighty power of God. We who were once dead weights, are now quickened unto life.

The Church as a Body

According to 1 Corinthians 12, the Church is also a living body. Because we are living cells, we are part of a body—the body of Christ, the living Church.

A body must have a life source to keep it from decomposing, and it must have a purpose. The Lord's living body on the earth is no longer a single, physical, visible body; it is a mighty, invisible, spiritual Body made of living cells—little temples all united under the Head.

In a building, the cornerstone is all important for stability. In a body, the all-important part is the head. The Church is a mighty, organized Body, but the Executive Head is Jesus. If He is not the brains, we will move far from our reason for being.

There is one Head, one Body, and one Spirit, so the invisible spiritual Church is *united*. There is also a unity in diversity. Our Lord recognizes the thousands of different gifts, works, and members that make His church the power that it is.

For a moment, let us look at the unity of the Body. In the physical sense, we recognize the Church as a visible organization. Organization is not a Spirit-quenching concept, but rather, another word for unity. In the physical church, Jesus Christ has given unity expressed through organization. He wants us to recognize and respect every part of the visible and invisible Body, and not scorn the differences.

One who knows and respects the working of a physical body will delight in the gift of the pancreas as much as in the gift of the respiratory system. The inner organs will be as highly respected as the outer parts. In the same way, the Church has been given many gifts, both physical and spiritual. The church of Jesus Christ is a body, an organization in both the spiritual and physical sense, with Christ as the Head. There are many parts and many gifts in the Church.

In the local church, we recognize the pastor as the spiritual leader under Christ. We also recognize other people who have unique gifts. Some have the gift of administration, others the gifts of helps, organization, and edification. We are all one in Christ, but we do not all do the same thing in the Body; otherwise, we would not have a completely functioning Body.

Many confuse the role of the Body and the functions of the Body. There is a sense in which the Body must be concerned about itself and its well-being, so it can fulfill its purpose. A person will take care of his physical body by nourishing it and seeing that it gets the proper amount of rest. There is nothing wrong with a strong body; it can accomplish more than a weak body. As members of the body of Christ, we should learn to appreciate administration and edification to the Body itself. We are to build up ourselves in the most holy faith and edify one another through the fruit of the Spirit and the gifts of the Spirit.

A body must have a life source. The Bible says the life source of our physical bodies is the blood. The life source of a spiritual body is the spirit, and in the case of the Church, it is the Holy Spirit. This is the very reason the Church cannot be destroyed by any of the forces of hell or earth. We are in the world, but we are not of the world, because the body of Christ is energized by the eternal Spirit.

I look at the local church as an organization that will either be a habitation of Satan or a habitation of the Holy Spirit. The Bible tells us clearly that the Antichrist will use the false church, which will be a religious organization. The logic is clear: the church without the Holy Spirit will become an instrument, or a body, for the Antichrist. We must choose to be filled with either the spirit of the age or the Spirit of God.

The Church is not to catch the spirit of this age,

but to correct it. We are to be concerned about what God is saying to this age, not what this age is saying about God. It is not this world that we need to know better; it is the other world. It is not the language of the streets, but the language of the Master.

In addition, it is necessary for a body to have a purpose. The Church does not exist on earth to be impressive. Too often the Church has been more interested in making an impression on the world, rather than being an influence on or a witness to the world.

The other day, I met a man who spends his life "pumping iron" (weight lifting). He is undoubtedly very much alive. He also has an impressive physique. But this magnificent specimen of manhood has not accomplished a thing in life. He is so wrapped up in being strong for beauty's sake, that he has no reason to be strong for goodness' sake.

Sam Shoemaker (who was instrumental in helping Alcoholics Anonymous develop their 12 steps to help alcoholics) once said: "Too much of organized religion looks backward for its credentials, like an old family of run-down aristocrats who like to remember the heroic deeds of long-dead ancestors." God doesn't want history; He wants availability.

I read of a man who attended a church and observed that each member of the congregation bowed toward a blank wall when leaving the sanctuary. When he asked some of them why they did this, they responded, "Because we've always done it." Their answer bothered him so much that he asked for, and finally received, permission to see what was behind the blank wall. After removing several coats of paint, he found a beautiful mosaic of

Jesus. The church had painted over Christ's portrait!

The world will think we're nuts if we worship a dead tradition, but they will receive life if we will proclaim a living Christ through the Body.

In the next chapter, we will learn that the mighty church of Jesus Christ exists for a purpose. We are to take our strong Body, empowered by the Holy Spirit, and evangelize the whole world. We are to be a tool for Jesus Christ, available to Him, built up in Him, and filled with Him for the purpose of tearing down the dominions of the devil and building the kingdom of God. We have not been baptized into Christ's body to look good, but to do good. Too many are like the lazy man who, after being saved, was heard to pray: "Oh Lord, use me, please use me—but use me in an advisory capacity!"

The Church as a Bride

The Church is also the bride of Christ and looks forward to that hour when she will be presented to the Bridegroom, as a glorious Church without spot or wrinkle.

What is the Church? It is a spiritual, eternal Building and a spiritual, eternal Body. But it is also a spiritual, eternal Bride with the glorious privilege of having an intimate relationship with Christ forever.

The most important thing about a bride and a bridegroom is their love for one another. The Church is God's love object on this earth. We are His treasure—the apple of His eye. But love must be reciprocal to find fulfillment. Thus, the Church must constantly express its love to Christ as its ultimate purpose. We gather to worship Him. It is our duty, as the bride of Christ, to love Him above all others. It is our duty, as His bride, to keep ourselves only for Him as His exclusive possession and to prepare ourselves for His sudden return.

Understanding what the Church is all about makes it obvious why one should desire to be part of the Church. Jesus is building His church. Satan is building his kingdom. You are part of either Christ's church or Satan's kingdom. You should be part of the Church because it gives not only security from sin, death, and hell, but also meaning and purpose to life right now. As part of His body, you have the joy of knowing your works will follow you with eternal rewards.

You should be part of the Church because it is the love object of God. In this eternal relationship as a bride, we can become perfected, without spot or wrinkle. Paul said: "Eye hath not seen, nor ear heard, neither have entered into the heart of man, the things which God hath prepared for them that love him" (1 Corinthians 2:9).

Since the Church means so much to Him, you should become a part of the invisible Church now, through a new birth from sin. Then join a visible church with all its blessings and responsibilities.

The Church is alive and well on planet earth. It's the only organization with a blessed hope, because her future is not based on what happens to this earth.

11

The Church Should Mind Its Own Business

The Ministry

A divinely called and scripturally ordained ministry has been provided by our Lord for the threefold purpose of leading the Church in: (1)Evangelization of the world (Mark 16:15-20), (2)Worship of God (John 4:23,24), (3)Building a body of saints being perfected in the image of His Son (Ephesians 4:11-16).

You are sitting in the doctor's office. Some time ago you felt an unusual pain in your lower stomach. After several weeks of growing concern, you submitted yourself to a battery of tests. Now you are waiting to hear the results of those tests.

The door opens, and your name is called. You face the doctor and hear him say, "I have some bad news to tell you. The tests were positive." "How long, doctor?" is your first question. "Not long," he answers.

From now on you will have to live with the reality of those two words in every waking moment. Those two words will change your life. Priorities will change, relationships will be adjusted, and activities will be altered. When we realize we don't have long, our whole perspective changes.

The Church has been receiving reports lately

through the Holy Spirit. In one sense, these reports are exciting and thrilling, but in another sense, their message is sobering and urgent. The Spirit of God is telling the Church it doesn't have long to remain on this earth. What we would do we must do quickly. The Church faces the crisis of limited time.

When time is short, it becomes incumbent upon us to be concerned about our real reason for being, our most vital duties, and our ultimate mission. Crisis times are times of heroism or cowardice, times of fear or faith, times of the best or the worst, and times of the greatest waste or the greatest gain.

The Church must determine its business on earth. Since you are a part of the Church, it is necessary for you to determine what your business is in the time the Church has left.

The purpose, ministry, and mission of the Church are threefold. They were symbolized in the tabernacle in the wilderness and in Solomon's Temple. The tabernacle and the temple had a three-part design: the Holy of Holies, the Holy Place, and the outer court.

The Church has a threefold ministry. The Holy of Holies depicts ministry to the Lord, the Holy Place depicts ministry to the body of Christ, and the outer court depicts ministry to the world. All three of these ministries are necessary; you can't have one without the other. It's like asking a person to decide which leg on a three-legged stool is the most important. First, we will look at the ministry that makes the other ministries meaningful and powerful.

Worship of God

The Church and its members exist to minister to

103

the Lord. This is the least understood and most neglected ministry in and through the church of Jesus Christ. It cannot be understood in terms of goals measured on the scales of human achievement; nor can it be placed on an organizational chart. It is a spiritual object, dimension, and revelation. It is comprehended only by those born of the Spirit, and even then it is often neglected.

One of the most succinct and profound statements in the Bible concerns worship: "God is a Spirit: and they that worship him must worship him in spirit and in truth" (John 4:24). In this one statement, the Holy Spirit has revealed the necessary elements in our ministry to the Lord. These elements are: the preeminence of God as the object of worship, the transcendence or spirituality of God as the dimension of worship, and the knowledge of God as the result of worship.

First, the quality of our worship is determined by the object of our worship. The first commandment of the Law was: "Thou shalt have no other gods before me" (Exodus 20:3). The New Testament puts it in the framework of a positive statement: "Thou shalt love the Lord thy God with all thy heart" (Matthew 22:37). The entire framework of spiritual truth is built on the preeminence of God himself. *God himself must be the object of ultimate value.* When it comes to worship, He is a jealous God. He must be preeminent. The Church cannot serve two masters. There must be no division of loyalties; no other authority must be allowed to take charge of the Church's business.

Elton Trueblood has pointed out how unique the number *one* is. There is a big difference between one and two, not in degree but in kind. However, the difference between two and three is slight. The man with three wives differs very little from the man with two. However, there is a vast difference between a man having one wife, being monogamous, and a man having two wives.

In light of the command to have no other gods before God, we are to be monogamous in our worship.

Do you know what true worship is? In the face of the superpowers of hell, in the face of the Russian Bear, in the face of the awesome threat of the Antichrist, the true worshiper—with all his body, soul, and spirit—says, "He is Lord; He is first. There is no other God; He is preeminent." Rather than knowing the Lord's will, it is more important to know the Lord. All our means must flow to this end. Our goal must be that Jesus Christ will be exalted and God will be glorified.

We must ask ourselves some questions: Is Jesus Christ everything in what we do? Why do we go to church? To see what God can do for us, or to see what God requires of us? Is Jesus glorified by our giving or our singing, or do we seek to share the glory? Why am I preaching? To fill the pulpit? To impress the people? Or to exalt the Lord Jesus that He might be all in all?

After recognizing the preeminence of God, we must move to the second element of worship: *the spirituality of God.* This simply means the true meaning of worship is not found in anything physical. The true worshiper is not dependent on posture, circumstance, or location. One of the greatest examples of this truth is found in the Book of Revelation. The apostle John was on the Isle of Patmos, banished by the emperor and separated from his friends. He was without any visible aids to worship, nevertheless he could write: "I was in the Spirit on the Lord's day" (Revelation 1:10).

The ultimate value of God cannot be understood by the human intellect, but only by the help of the Holy Spirit. This is the reason we must be filled with the Spirit—that our worship will not be hindered by the things of the flesh, and all things can be used to the glory of God.

If God is the object of ultimate value, and we are able, through the new birth, to worship Him in Spirit, then we will have a *true knowledge of God.* This is the result of true worship: The Church will know its God. Any church that knows the Lord will have a power beyond all the resources of earth. The New Testament doesn't say, "Ye shall know the rules and by them ye are bound," but rather, "Ye shall know the truth" (John 8:32). The greatest thing that could be said about a church is: "They know their God." If we are not sure of God, we will be unsure of everything we do.

Why did the Early Church have such authority? They were sure of their God. They had faith to invade the enemy's territory because they knew God is greater than anything or anybody in the world. *The Church needs to redefine everything in the light of the knowledge of God.*

But God will only reveal himself to true worshipers, to those who have pure motives and who recognize Him as the object of ultimate value who transcends the material.

Edification of the Body

The Church and its members exist to minister to

the body of Christ. The true worshiper will seek a strong ministry to the Body.

After we are sure of our God, we will be sure of ourselves. For too long the Church has taken a defensive stand in justifying its existence. It is time for the Church to shake off its sick self-image and its inferiority complex. God intended the Church to be an army, the mighty Spirit-energized body of Christ, a glorious force for God, which the gates of hell cannot prevail against. Nowhere does the Bible counsel the Church to be weak. On the contrary, God has supplied the Church with mighty weapons and supernatural resources to make it strong.

In their ministry to God's house, the priests concentrated on three things: the altar, the shewbread, and the lampstand. If we are going to be strong, we must concentrate on the truths that are symbolized by these tabernacle articles.

First, the altar of incense, symbolizing *righteous praise,* was lit with fire from the bronze altar of judgment. It conveyed the message that God was accepting the adoration of His people. In ministry to each other, members of the body of Christ are to constantly encourage one another in forgiveness, based on the sacrifice of Christ, which is typified by the bronze altar.

But this is just the beginning. Now the Church may enter His gates with thanksgiving and go into His courts with praise. In order for a church to be strong, there must be constant praise and gratitude for one another based on divine pardon. We are strong in the Lord because we are forgiven. We are strong in *gratitude*—not pride. The joy of the Lord and the edification that comes through praise are a great source of our strength.

Second, the table of shewbread, symbolizing the staff of life, typifies the living Bread—food for the soul. The strong church is not just a society of grateful redeemed ones, but a living body that needs constant *nourishment*. We are to build ourselves up through the ministry of the Word: "Man shall not live by bread alone, but by every word that proceedeth out of the mouth of God" (Matthew 4:4).

The pot of manna in the Holy of Holies symbolizes Jesus, the Bread of Life. But there was also the daily ministration of bread in the Holy Place, which depicts the need for the bread of the Word. What is learned at the beginning of life is learned for life, and this is true of the second birth. If a church is to be strong, it must be strong in adoration based on forgiveness, but it must also minister the Word. "The words that I speak unto you," said Jesus, "they are spirit, and they are life" (John 6:63).

Third, there was the golden candlestick. Everything done in ministry to God's house was illuminated by the golden candlestick, which symbolizes the Holy Spirit. If a church is going to be strong, it must give emphasis to the *Holy Spirit*. After all, the Church has been given the Holy Spirit for the purpose of making it strong in character (the fruit of the Spirit) and strong in spiritual abilities (the gifts of the Spirit). The life of the body of Christ is in the Holy Spirit. This is the fundamental reason our church chooses to put such great emphasis on all the ministries of the Spirit.

The lampstand supported seven lamps. The strong church will seek to allow all the channels to be open so the church will be aglow with the revelation of heaven.

The church needs to be sure of itself in God. A

weak body has limited abilities and service. We are to build ourselves up, to edify and be edified. We need to minister to each other. This is another reason why the believer must be faithful in his attendance at the house of God.

Evangelization of the World

The Church and its members exist *to minister to the world.* The temple and tabernacle had an outer court where the altar of burnt offering stood. The laver was for cleansing and symbolized the truth that all may come through the shedding of blood and the cleansing of water by the Word.

What is the Church's ministry to the world? To proclaim the *good news* of the gospel that whosoever will may come. The Word of life must be proclaimed. There is power in the Blood and cleansing by the Word.

There are a thousand good causes in the world in which one may become involved. Each Christian should seek to become involved in being a witness. The role of the Church, as far as the world is concerned, is to constantly remember the Great Commission: We must go into the outer court of this world and proclaim the gospel to every creature, baptizing them in the name of the Father, Son, and Holy Spirit.

The Church should concentrate on its own business! There is always the temptation to substitute good works for the *good news,* or to substitute salvation by a multitude of ways and means. If salvation cannot come through proclaiming Jesus Christ in the power of the Spirit, then there is no hope. "There is none other name under heaven given among men, whereby we must be saved" (Acts 4:12). It is the Church's job to seek and to save the lost, to help win their souls to Christ.

When we are sure of God, we will be sure not only of ourselves, but also of our mission. True worship is not lip service, but life service. Historically, whenever churches have lost the wonder of God, the supernatural God, they have begun to doubt His power and ability. They have seen man from a carnal viewpoint and have sought carnal means to save him. But man is more than a beast; he is a living soul.

When addressing a religious conference, Hudson Taylor told how he had seen a Chinese boy fall overboard and drown. The tragedy, he said, was in the fact that none of the fishermen had come to the aid of the drowning lad because it was inconvenient for them. And Taylor had been unable to offer them enough money in his frantic efforts to persuade them to do something.

The audience was aghast. Sensing their indignation, Taylor quietly said, "Is the body then of so much more value than the soul? We condemn the fishermen. We say they are guilty of the boy's death because they could have easily saved him, but chose not to. But what of the millions whom we leave to perish by apathy, indifference, or misguided priorities?"

Here is the crux of the matter: The world will only be saved through Jesus Christ; that is the only way of salvation the Church can offer. There are a million good deeds to be done and a million projects to take up our time. But until every person has heard the gospel in the power of the Spirit, and every soul has been saved by the cleansing of the Blood, the Church's ministry to the world must be to proclaim the gospel. Any other effort is secondary and disastrous.

Suppose a man has been bitten by a snake and is dying in filth and squalor. At the same time, he doesn't have any food and he has a multitude of other needs. In your hand is the antidote for his snakebite. Are you going to say, "He will not be receptive to the antidote until we give him food. He will not listen until we get him better housing. He will not understand unless we give him an education first!"? No! A full stomach, adequate housing, and a Ph.D. won't do a thing for him until the antidote for death is received.

The Church is the depository of the antidote for sin. God has given us the Great Commission to administer that antidote to the world. Then and only then can the Church become involved in other priorities.

The Church's ministry is threefold, and it is vital that all three ministries be functioning in balance or the Church's entire reason for being will fail. If the Church ministers only to the Lord, it will become weak and the world will be lost. If the Church ministers only to the world, it will become lost and lose its relationship with God. If the Church ministers only to its own house, it will lose the supreme object of worship, and the world will lose sight of its Saviour.

The Church has a divinely called and ordained ministry. We don't have long, but we do have time to minister to the Lord, to ourselves, and to our world. With that kind of ministry, the gates of hell will not be able to prevail.

12

Faith Healers—
Con Artists or Christ Exalters?

Divine Healing

Divine healing is an integral part of the gospel. Deliverance from sickness is provided for in the Atonement, and is the privilege of all believers (Isaiah 53:4,5; Matthew 8:16,17; James 5:14-16).

Something tragic has taken place in the name of God. The great Biblical doctrine of divine healing has been so abused that many have abandoned its benefits; resulting in a loss to the Church and a victory for the devil.

There is a parallel between this doctrine and that of the baptism in the Holy Spirit with the evidence of speaking in other tongues. In both cases, many people have seen the excesses and failures of the personalities involved and have chosen to throw out these Biblical doctrines entirely. While we should be aware of the incorrect reactions of some in response to these Biblical promises, we also need to understand the Biblical principles that will enable us to react scripturally to God's promises.

In the first part of this chapter, we will identify errors surrounding divine healing. In the second part, we will deal with the scriptural principles, patterns, and promises in the doctrine of divine healing.

Errors Concerning Divine Healing

1. *The gifts of healing were a temporary sign gift to establish the authority of the apostles, but spiritual gifts no longer play a role in the Church.* This concept has absolutely no basis in Scripture. On the contrary, we are encouraged to seek earnestly the best gifts.

Throughout the Bible, we are given the principle of divine healing. The prophet Joel said in the last days God would pour out His Spirit, resulting in a special outpouring of divine power through faith (Joel 2:28,29). According to James, part of the elders' role in the church is to pray and anoint the sick with oil for the purpose of divine healing. Healing of the sick is one of the signs Jesus said would follow believers (Mark 16:17,18). There is no scriptural evidence that Jesus Christ has revoked the promise of divine healing, any more than there is proof that He has rescinded the gift of eternal life.

Why do people claim some of God's promises in the New Testament and in the same breath deny others? Those who believe and practice divine healing for the glory of God are seeing people healed in spite of men's honest and sincere misinterpretations. Jesus is still in the healing business. The day of miracles is not past.

2. *It is God's will for me to be sick.* The Bible teaches that the physical body is corrupt or mortal because of sin. Sin brought a blight and a curse upon this world. Thorns, thistles, and other evidences of the curse appeared. But it is not God's will for His people to live under the curse. In fact, He is building a city where there is no curse. He is not willing that any should perish. If it were God's will for people to

be sick, while Jesus was on earth He would have laid hands on well people and made them sick.

William Caldwell relates the following incident:

"Following a service in one church, a man whom I knew to be a Christian visiting from a distant city approached me with another man. After the introduction he said, 'Brother Caldwell, this man is also a Christian. Will you pray for him to be healed?'

"Immediately the man exclaimed almost in horror, 'No, don't pray for me to be healed. I don't believe it is God's will to heal. If you prayed and God healed me against His will, it would be an awful thing. It is better that I remain sick.'

"Trying to help him, I pointed out: 'The Lord "forgiveth all thine iniquities; [and] healeth all thy diseases" (Psalm 103:3), thereby treating sin and sickness with equal terms. Furthermore, Jesus says: "These signs shall follow *them that believe;* . . . they shall lay hands on the sick, and they shall recover" (Mark 16:17,18).'

"But no, the man was firm in his idea that it was not God's will to heal. 'Well,' I asked him, 'what do you do when you are sick?' He replied, 'I do the sensible thing, of course. I go to the doctor.' At that it was my turn to express horror. 'What? You are so sure God wants you to be sick, yet you go to the doctor and get him involved in a conspiracy against God!' If it were not God's will that the sick be healed, then every doctor and nurse would be an enemy of God's will and every hospital an offense against God." (William Caldwell, *Meet the Healer* [Tulsa, OK: Miracle Moments Evangelistic Assoc., Inc., 1965], p. 24.)

3. *Everyone should be healed right now because healing is in the Atonement.* The atonement of

Jesus Christ paid for the redemption of mankind. He took our punishment and suffered so we could be healed. He shed His blood and died to complete the perfect work of redemption. Jesus Christ conquered Satan and arose as the firstfruits of those who die in Christ (1 Corinthians 15:20).

He forgave our sins by His sacrifice, but our redeemed souls are still dwelling in unredeemed bodies. We do, however, have the promise that one day we will have redeemed or glorified bodies. Romans 8:23 tells us: "We ourselves . . . groan inwardly as we wait eagerly for our adoption as sons, the redemption of our bodies" (NIV).

Jesus Christ provided for our complete and eternal salvation on Calvary, signaled by His cry, "It is finished" (John 19:30). We can claim the redemption of our souls—total forgiveness from sin. Jesus Christ also provided complete and eternal healing for our bodies, but no one presently living on this planet has yet received a glorified body. No one on this earth has been totally removed from the consequences of the curse.

Did the sacrifice on Calvary provide for a perfect work or a partial work? Jesus Christ provided for the *total* redemption of everything lost by sin. We claim that finished work for our souls, our bodies, and our world. The perfect work of Christ has delivered us from the consequences of sin, is delivering us, and will deliver us. By the same token, we believe His work on Calvary has healed us, is healing us, and will heal us. His sacrifice has redeemed our world from the curse of the devil, is redeeming our world, and will redeem our world.

When we say, "Healing is in the Atonement," we must remember that we have not yet seen the *ultimate* healing. Even those who have been miraculously healed have not been perfectly healed as yet. Salvation has come through Calvary, but we have not yet realized perfection in our body, soul, spirit, or world.

4. *All sickness is a result of sin in the one who is sick.* This statement stems from not understanding that we live in a dangerous, sick world, and that we have salvation's treasure in earthen vessels. To say that all sickness is a result of the curse is Biblical, but to say that all sickness is a result of sin in the person who is sick is not scriptural. Furthermore, it brings condemnation and accusations from the devil. Sickness might be a result of the consequences of sin, but nowhere did Jesus limit sickness to being the result of unconfessed sin. The story of the blind man should make that clear.

> His disciples asked him, saying, Master, who did sin, this man, or his parents, that he was born blind? Jesus answered, Neither hath this man sinned, nor his parents: but that the works of God should be made manifest in him (John 9:2,3).

If all sickness were a result of unconfessed sin, every time the Christian confessed sin in his life, known or unknown, he would be instantly healed. Such teaching brings condemnation and plays people right into the devil's hand. It causes the believer to doubt his salvation and puts him in a place of failure through self, rather than a place of victory through Christ.

5. *All faith healers are con artists.* From the beginning we must clearly state that no man is a divine healer or a faith healer. To be technically accurate, we should probably call the legitimate

faith healer a "faith builder" or a "Christ exalter," because *only Christ heals.*

Jesus Christ has given many gifts to the Church. He has given pastors, teachers, and evangelists, as well as spiritual gifts. God has chosen unique men and ministries to edify the body of Christ. Some of these people have been given an extraordinary ability to build faith for healing through the Word. I resent anyone placing a whole group of people in one category, then dismissing the whole lot because of an unscrupulous few. There are legitimate God-given faith builders in His church.

To our sorrow, it is obvious that there are also men and women who are con artists. The Bible clearly says there will be those who will stand before the Throne and ask for entrance into heaven because they have healed the sick and cast out devils in His name. But God will tell them they are iniquitous workers and He never had anything to do with them (Matthew 7:22,23). *When God confirms His Word, He does not necessarily confirm the personality or ministry that brings the Word.*

The Bible admonishes us to know those who minister among us for our own God-given protection. We should be more concerned about a man's character than about his claims. The devil wants to set us all up for the Antichrist by tempting us to follow men whose claim to fame is performing miracles rather than living the Christlike life. Beware of anyone who asks for your allegiance. No man can be a substitute for your own faith in the Man of Galilee.

The Scriptural Basis for Divine Healing

Now that we have reviewed some errors and

misunderstandings surrounding divine healing, we will examine the scriptural basis for divine healing.

1. *The person of God.* It is within God's character to heal. As a matter of fact, one of the names of God is *Jehovah-Rapha,* or "The Lord that healeth."

When the Word became flesh and dwelt among us, He healed the sick. Since it is the very nature of God to heal, it stands to reason that when He became flesh, He would heal in the flesh. The record of Jesus is a long parade of miracles. He had power not only to forgive sins, but also to heal the sick. There are accounts in Scripture where Jesus healed all who were afflicted.

Jesus performed an amazing variety of healing miracles. The divine Healer set people free from every incurable disease known to man. No sickness stymied His ability to heal. The blind received their sight, the dumb spoke, and the lame and paralyzed were given strong, healthy limbs. The awful scourge of leprosy was lifted time and again, the high fever was checked and the temperature returned to normal, the issue of blood was dried up by a touch, and the withered hand was stretched out and made whole. Funeral processions were interrupted and changed to resurrection parades, the demons of hell were evicted from their habitations, and epileptic seizures were silenced.

This same Jesus is alive today. He is the same yesterday, today, and forever. In Matthew 28:20, He said, "Lo, I am with you alway."

2. *The promise of God.* We have sound, scriptural reasons for believing in divine healing. When Jesus gave His disciples the Great Commission, He also gave them the *power* to cast out demons and heal all manner of sickness. Jesus said, "I give unto you

power" (Luke 10:19). The word "power" here is the word *dunamis*—the same power given to the Church at Pentecost, and the same power He has promised to His church in all ages.

Jesus gave the disciples the *authority* to use His name; it was His power of attorney. When someone is given the power of attorney, he is authorized by that person to act in his place. Jesus Christ has given believers the authority to use His name in His place, during His physical absence. He has given power and authority to those who believe (Mark 16:17,18).

In Nazareth, Jesus himself could not do great works because of the people's unbelief (Matthew 13:58). Can you imagine what would happen if every believer began to reach out in faith and believe the promise of God? Can you imagine what power would be generated and the authority that would be exercised?

Jesus also promised healing through the anointing of oil and the laying on of hands:

> Is any sick among you? Let him call for the elders of the church; and let them pray over him, anointing him with oil in the name of the Lord: and the prayer of faith shall save the sick, and the Lord shall raise him up (James 5:14,15).

That promise doesn't sound like our Healer has decided to resign. The true Church is the church of Jesus Christ, and through that Church comes provision for healing in and to the Body.

Jesus also provided gifts of healing to benefit the human body. When God answers prayer, He often uses the natural functions of the body to restore healing. He starts a trend toward health rather than sickness—this is a gift of healing. However, there are times when He chooses to supersede the natural healing process and instantly makes the person whole—this is a miracle of healing.

3. *The pattern of divine healing.* God's pattern of divine healing was established in the New Testament Church and follows the teaching of our Lord Jesus. The purpose and object of healing is not to avoid a problem or to relieve pain, but to bring glory and honor to Jesus. The fundamental reason for healing is the same as the reason for the gift of the Holy Spirit: to make Jesus known. Often we may have asked for healing to further our plans, to satisfy the desire to be free from pain, or to avoid problems in our lives, rather than seeking to advance His kingdom. But if we will seek healing to bring glory to Jesus, *then He will heal for His glory.*

The means of healing is through faith. You cannot be good enough, and you cannot work hard enough for it. The means is faith, and the object is Jesus. God has provided, but faith is the means whereby we take what God has promised and act accordingly. Faith is a willingness to believe God. At this moment, healing is provided through the Healer. Look at Him, forget yourself, and reach out and touch the Word.

The methods of healing are not limited. We see the pattern in the Early Church. The disciples exercised faith by a simple word and command. People were healed through fasting and prayer. People were healed by anointing handkerchiefs and aprons with oil. People were healed when Peter's shadow passed over them. People were healed by the laying on of hands. What is the Word trying to communicate? God will use any method, but it is up to us to simply exercise faith in His name and for His glory.

13

The Jesus Rally
None of Us Will Ever Forget

The Blessed Hope

The resurrection of those who have fallen asleep in
Christ and their translation together with those who
are alive and remain unto the coming of the Lord is
the imminent and blessed hope of the Church
(1 Thessalonians 4:16,17; Romans 8:23; Titus 2:13;
1 Corinthians 15:51,52).

Jesus Christ is the Author and Finisher of our
faith, but we are the children of reason. Faith sees
the end as well as the beginning. Reason sees only
the process, and struggles in its limitations. The
blessed hope triumphs over the darkness and gloom
of reason through the victory of our faith, which is
Jesus Christ. Who can reason out the resurrection of
the dead and the rapture of the living saints?
Reason must bow to faith and accept an authority
above the imperfect rationale of man.

The blessed hope is a living hope because it comes
from the Lord himself.

A missionary was trying to explain to a group of
Moslems why he trusted in Christ. "Let us
imagine," said the missionary, "that we are walking
along a road and the road comes to a fork. We do not
know which road to take. We seek a guide, and we
find two. One guide is dead, and the other is alive.

Which one would you ask for directions?" The Moslems answered in unison, "The living one, of course." Then the missionary paused and said with deep emotion, "Why would you ask me to follow a dead Muhammad when I can follow the living Christ?"

Christ's Second Coming

We believe in the blessed hope because the Author and Finisher of our faith has declared it, shown it, and commanded us to look for it. The Scriptures resound with the promise of our Lord. He said He will come again *in person*: "I go to prepare a place for you. And if I go . . . I will come again, and receive you unto myself; that where I am, there ye may be also" (John 14:2,3).

In His great prophetic teachings, Jesus repeatedly assured us He will return: "And when these things begin to come to pass, then look up, and lift up your heads; for your redemption draweth nigh" (Luke 21:28). The angel of the Lord proclaimed it at the time of our Lord's ascension: "This same Jesus, which is taken up from you into heaven, shall so come in like manner as ye have seen him go into heaven" (Acts 1:11). The apostles taught it: "For the Lord himself shall descend from heaven with a shout" (1 Thessalonians 4:16). We look for the blessed hope and appearing of our Lord and Saviour.

The fact of Christ's literal, personal, and imminent return is substantiated without question by the Lord himself, emphasized in Scripture, and confirmed throughout the ages by the quickening revelation of the Holy Spirit. He has told us He will come *on time*—God's time. He came right on schedule the first time, that the Scriptures might be fulfilled. By the omnipotent hand of God, the whole world was moved to make possible that moment when, in the "fullness of time," His Son would come from heaven. But God has another moment planned that is kept secret in the councils of heaven; no man knows the day or the hour. Jesus will come in the twinkling of an eye at that divinely appointed moment.

Everything around us seems out of control. To view this world from a human viewpoint is enough to cause our hearts to fail for fear. But to those who are looking for the Lord to return, everything is being moved into place by the sovereignty of God for Christ's return. We are now living in the "fullness of time," as it relates to the end of the world.

Why are men's hearts failing them for fear? Because their hope is not a blessed hope. Rather, it is a fragile thing held together by tenuous agreements between nations, the fate of economics, and the uncertainty of life. But we are not people of a dying hope, a rudderless ship, or a leaderless kingdom. Everything is under control. The nations are in place. The celestial trumpet player is standing poised for the final announcement.

Christ is coming not only in person and on time, but also *in power*. He is no longer the meek and lowly Nazarene. He is the Lion of Judah, the King of kings, the Creator God. No force on earth or in hell can stop the coming of Jesus Christ.

The return of our Lord will be in two phases, but we are going to limit the scope of this chapter to the first phase or event: the coming of Jesus Christ for the Church. This is called the Rapture. According to the apostle Paul, Jesus will descend to call His bride, and while He is still in the air, the believers

123

will be taken up to meet Him (1 Thessalonians 4:16,17).

The return of Christ is imminent; meaning, He could come at any moment. His coming will directly affect two groups of people: the dead in Christ, and those who are alive in Christ. The dead are going to rise first. Throughout history, man has wondered, "If a man die, shall he live again?" (Job 14:14). The greatest minds have wrestled with this question. Without Christ, the mystery would still be locked in silence, and the cold fear of the unknown would continue to paralyze the stoutest heart.

But Christ is risen from the dead. This fact in itself has been the theme of almost 2,000 Easters. But even more wonderful is how the resurrection of Jesus affects our loved ones. The Bible says Jesus Christ has "become the firstfruits of them that slept" (1 Corinthians 15:20). In other words, those who die in Christ are not dead. Their bodies are asleep, but their souls (the real person) are immediately with the Lord. This is a great comfort. Death cannot separate us from our Lord.

The Bible removes all the mystery when it tells us that "to die is gain" (Philippians 1:21). To die is to be with the Lord. We are not merely a body; our body is only a treasure chest holding that most precious possession—our soul. At death there is a separation of the soul from the body.

An atheistic doctor was talking to a believer one day. "I've done many an autopsy on dead bodies," said he, "but I have never seen a living soul." The believer quietly replied, "Would you expect to find a living soul in a dead body? Even if it had been there, no human eye has been constructed to see the invisible."

But the blessed hope is not limited to the invisible, eternal soul. God's plan of redemption includes the final triumph of everything that was lost through sin, including our physical bodies.

The Resurrection of the Body

To help us understand the meaning of death in relationship to the Rapture, our Lord taught in parables. He used the familiar to lead us to the unfamiliar. He compared physical death to the planting of a seed.

To me, planting a seed in the ground is one of the least productive and most difficult tasks in farming. Yet, I have never seen a farmer who is sowing seed and, at the same time, weeping because he has lost the seed. On the contrary, the farmer is usually happy because he is planting the seed in *faith*. He can say to skeptics and unbelievers, "You may think I'm crazy, but do you see this little seed? I'm going to put this kernel of wheat in the ground and cover it with dirt. In a few days it will lose its covering and die. But it will also begin a process that will set it free from the limitations of its shell. And eventually, it will grow into a tall stalk and be laden down with grain."

You may say, "I know that; everyone does." But what if you had never witnessed the miracle of springtime and harvest? You would probably react just as the unbeliever does toward death. To him it is all over; death is the ultimate separation, the tragic end to a farce called life. But to the believer, in spite of sorrow for the temporary separation, there is faith, because Jesus has become the "firstfruits" of the believing dead (1 Corinthians 15:20).

125

What are "firstfruits"? They are simply the guarantee of a similar product in the future. If we want to know what is going to happen to us, we should look to Jesus—He passed through death to bring us life.

For centuries, Christians have died and been planted like seeds in the earth. But someday the trumpet of the Lord will announce the fulfillment of the harvest, and the miracle will happen: the dead will be resurrected.

The Bible says that we are "sown." The sowing is the only part we have seen. But the Scriptures also say we will be raised. First Corinthians 15:42-44 contrasts the sowing and the resurrection of the body.

1. The body is sown in corruption, but it will be raised in *incorruption*. No matter how we try to prevent it, our bodies are in a constant state of decay. Paul felt the impact of this truth when he cried, "Who shall deliver me from the body of this death?" (Romans 7:24).

A cancer patient some time ago said to me, "There are times when I wish I could tear the insidious growth from my body. I feel it working, and I want to make it stop." Our bodies are corrupt; they are mortal. Like seeds, they will eventually be put into the ground, but someday they will be raised in incorruption. When the dead in Christ are resurrected, we will have new bodies that will never deteriorate.

2. The body is sown in dishonor, but it will be raised in *glory*. How often we weep over our sins and failures. We are reminded of the store that was having a sale. The sign over the bargain counter read: "Merchandise soiled—greatly reduced in

price." We are sown with a record of dishonorable conduct, but we will be raised to honor in the house of God; He will present us faultless before the Throne.

3. The body is sown in weakness, but it will be raised in *power*. "The spirit indeed is willing, but the flesh is weak" (Matthew 26:41). I am astounded at my weaknesses—the weakness of my mind, will, and purpose, and my lack of discipline. I try, but then grow weary of trying. We are sown in weakness, but we will be raised in the power of the Holy Spirit, never again to struggle against the weakness of self and the flesh.

4. The body is sown as a natural body, but it will be raised as a *spiritual* body. In this statement we have the summation. We are corrupt, dishonorable, and weak because we are in a natural body. The first Adam was made a living soul, but he sold us into death, and our body became a tomb. But the second Adam, Christ, became a quickening Spirit. When the Rapture takes place, the seed that has been sown in death will spring to full and glorious life.

The farmer does not weep as he sows the grain, nor does he forget about the grain after he has sown it. With watchful eye and constant care he tends the fields until harvesttime. It is a comfort to realize the Lord knows all those who are His, whether they are dead or alive. Not one will be lost, for the believer dies in Christ.

Death is also likened to sleep. Sleep, as you know, is for the tired, weary, or sick. It allows the body to remain still and quiet, although the real person is still very much alive. When we sleep our bodies are "dead to the world"—but this is a temporary state. Normally our bodies are awakened by a mechanism

127

within, or by the sound of an alarm clock. We go to sleep to be refreshed for a new day. We go to sleep in the dark and awaken to a new morning.

A little girl thought her bedroom was haunted and refused to sleep in it. One night her elder brother said, "Suzy, I'm going to settle this nonsense. I'm going to sleep in your room." "Oh no," she said, "please don't. The devil will get you." But he persisted, and the next morning he walked out of her room smiling; showing his little sister there was nothing to fear.

Jesus, our Elder Brother, was aware of man's fear of the grave. So for 3 days and nights, He "slept" in the place of the dead. Then on a glorious Sunday morning, He arose to exclaim: "I am he that liveth, and was dead; and, behold, I am alive forevermore, Amen; and have the keys of hell and of death" (Revelation 1:18).

Because of His triumph, when we say farewell to loved ones who have died in the faith, we can have hope. We have a hope that "maketh not ashamed." It is a blessed hope, because it is a *certain* hope.

The Nature of the Rapture

The blessed hope of the Church involves more than the dead in Christ. First Thessalonians 4:17 says: "We which are alive and remain shall be caught up together with them in the clouds." It would be well for us to remember the nature of the Rapture.

1. The Rapture is a *catching away*. The Greek word used here, *harpazo*, means to seize hastily; to draw to oneself by swift, sudden movement; and to rob with violence.

For 2,000 years, the church of Jesus Christ has

faced strong opposition. In the future, however, we will see an outpouring of satanic activity that will exceed anything known in Church history. This world is willingly following the "spirit of antichrist." It is still the grand design of Satan to overcome the overcomers. Through deception and evil men, he will do his best to defeat the Church. But about the time the councils of hell appear to be destroying the Church, the Lord will come in the clouds of glory and rapture the Church, robbing it from Satan and drawing it to himself in one swift movement.

2. The Rapture is a *catching up*. All believers—living and dead—will be caught up together to meet the Lord in the air (1 Thessalonians 4:16,17). It seems appropriate that the uniting of the body of Christ with the Head of the Church will take place in the devil's territory. For too long Satan has paraded as the "prince of the power of the air" (Ephesians 2:2). But, as believers, we can take comfort in knowing our Lord is building His church, and the councils of hell will not prevail against it.

3. The Rapture is a transfiguration and *transformation*. In a moment, in the twinkling of an eye, we will be clothed with immortality. Our bodies will be made like unto His own glorious body.

Lessons From the Rapture

What lessons should we learn from the truth of the Rapture?

1. *We must be ready.* It is awesome to think of those who will be left behind. The Bible tells us "one shall be taken, and the other left. Two men shall be in the field; the one shall be taken, and the other left" (Luke 17:35,36). No earthly loves or pressures

should deter us from a state of readiness. Jesus the King is coming soon.

How do you know if you are ready? If you have put your sins under the blood of Christ, and have turned away from them and are living for God, then you will be ready.

2. *We must be diligent in service.* Our Lord has commanded us to occupy until He comes. Every minute of time we give, and every dollar we invest, should be done to the glory of God, in expectation of our Lord's return.

The Bible says the blessed hope causes men to purify themselves. How? By doing things only to please Christ, and not for earthly gain or applause. If we really believe He's coming soon, what the world thinks and the few trinkets that we may gather will not mean much. Only what we do for Christ will last for eternity.

3. *We must be faithful to our coming Bridegroom.* We must live a life-style befitting the children of God; avoiding the sin and the contamination of a sin-sick world. We must be faithful in our witness. Do we witness of self, or of Christ? We must be faithful to a body of believers: "Not forsaking the assembling of ourselves together, . . . so much the more, as ye see the day approaching" (Hebrews 10:25).

4. *Most of all, we must be faithful in our love.* We must not allow the world to press us into its mold. We must not lose the qualities of our first love. Worship and adoration should be our greatest glory.

As we anticipate Christ's coming, we must be ready to meet Him, diligent in service, faithful unto death, and love without measure. "Even so, come, Lord Jesus" (Revelation 22:20).

14

When the World Comes Under New Management

The Millennial Reign of Christ

The second coming of Christ includes the rapture of the saints, which is our blessed hope, followed by the visible return of Christ with His saints to reign on the earth for 1,000 years (Zechariah 14:5; Matthew 24:27,30; Revelation 1:7; 19:11-14; 20:1-6). This millennial reign will bring the salvation of national Israel (Ezekiel 37:21,22; Zephaniah 3:19,20; Romans 11:26,27) and the establishment of universal peace (Isaiah 11:6-9; Psalm 72:3-8; Micah 4:3,4).

We cannot overestimate the importance of Israel in the plan of God. Not only is Israel a key to the events swirling about us at this moment, but also, an understanding of the divine covenants made with Israel is vital.

All Bible students know that God made everlasting and unconditional promises to Abraham, Isaac, Jacob, Moses, David, and others. It is a mistake to forget or ignore the covenants of God. While it is a temptation for us to think only of the promises God has made to the Church, we must also grasp the significance of Israel's role. The Church and Israel are so interrelated in God's program that the Church is identified as "spiritual Israel."

For many centuries, God used the nation of Israel

to fulfill His divine purpose on the earth. Through Israel, God revealed himself as the one true God and gave man His moral law. He taught them great spiritual truths that previously had been unknown. In the beginning, God ruled directly over Israel through a form of government called a *theocracy*. God himself directed the political fortunes of Israel through judges and prophets. When the people rebelled, God allowed them to have a king. This transition from a theocracy to a monarchy set in motion the events that culminated in the demise of Israel as a nation for hundreds of years.

The coming of the Messiah through the genealogy of Abraham and David was another turning point for Israel. Jesus came as promised and presented himself to His people as their Messiah. But the Bible records some of the most solemn words ever written as an indictment against Israel for their failure to receive Christ as the Messiah: "He [Jesus] came unto his own [Israel], and his own received him not. But as many as received him, to them gave he power to become the sons of God" (John 1:11,12).

God wanted the Jews to be not only the sons of Abraham but also the sons of God. He wanted to continue revealing His truth through Israel, but they did not choose to receive the truth; they rejected Him. God had no choice but to turn to the Gentiles to make them the depository of truth and use them to fulfill His purpose to the world. God has been fulfilling His promises and spreading His message through the empowered Church for the last 2,000 years. However, recent world events tell us clearly that the Church Age is about to end. The rapture of the Church is upon us. But God will *never* be finished with this world. He will keep His covenants not only with His church, but also with Israel.

The Reign of the Antichrist

After the rapture of the Church, the removal of the Holy Spirit, as we know His ministry today, will occur. The times of the Gentiles will be fulfilled and God will again use Israel to work out His purposes and will on the earth.

The Antichrist will rise in power to dominate world politics. For a time, Israel will make a treaty with the Antichrist, but midway through his reign, the Jews will recognize him as the false messiah. In spite of terrible persecution, Israel will stand against the beast during the Tribulation, and God will protect many of the Jews and bring them through this dreadful period. God's people have always been in opposition to the "spirit of antichrist" (1 John 4:3). The Church is now the standard against the "spirit of antichrist," but when the Church is gone, Israel will be the opposition to the Antichrist and will become the witness to the true Christ.

The Bible tells us at the end of the Antichrist's rule, the armies of the world will gather to do battle in a place called Armageddon.

The very word *Armageddon* sends a cold chill through the soul. Who will triumph in this titanic struggle? Before the armies engage in battle, the earth will tremble and the heavens will fold back like a scroll to reveal the most spectacular event in all history. The Bible says the whole earth will see the Son of Man. Revelation 19:11-15 gives us an inspiring account of this event.

And I saw heaven opened, and behold a white horse; and he that sat upon him was called Faithful and True, and in righteousness he doth judge and make war. His eyes were as a flame of fire, and on his head were many crowns; and he had a name written, that no man knew, but he himself. And he was clothed with a vesture dipped in blood: and his name is called The Word of God. And the armies which were in heaven followed him upon white horses, clothed in fine linen, white and clean. And out of his mouth goeth a sharp sword, that with it he should smite the nations; and he shall rule them with a rod of iron: and he treadeth the winepress of the fierceness and wrath of Almighty God.

God will keep His Word. The kingdoms of this world will become the kingdom of our God and of His Christ. Christ will reign in power on the earth.

However, before the Lord takes over the levers of earthly government, something else will happen. The Lord will direct a mighty angel to take hold of that old serpent, the devil—the father of lies, the accuser of the brethren, the deceiver of the nations—and cast him into the bottomless pit. Satan will be imprisoned for 1,000 years during the glorious reign of Jesus Christ and His millennial kingdom. Although Christ's millennial reign absorbs many pages of prophecy in the Bible, it is often neglected by Bible scholars. The purpose of this chapter is to whet appetites and revive interest in this incredible period of time.

Views of the Millennium

What is the Millennium? The answer can be found to a certain extent in the name itself. The word is taken from two Latin words: *mille,* translated "a thousand," and *annus,* meaning "one year." Thus, we are dealing with a 1,000-year period of time.

For some reason, a lot of people have a hard time believing the Word of God when it comes to the Millennium. They find it difficult to accept the tremendous prophecies of the Word in the literal sense, so they have chosen some interesting interpretations.

One group believes the Millennium will take place before the rapture of the Church. These people are identified as postmillennialists. A few questions will help us to determine whether their position is right or wrong: If we have already gone through the Millennium, when was the 1,000 years of worldwide peace? Can you say the world is growing better? When did every eye see Jesus? How is Christ going to come with His saints to rule and reign if they have not gone to meet Him? It is obvious that postmillennialism is not scripturally correct.

Another group teaches that there will not be a literal Millennium. They spiritualize the teaching of the Millennium. These people are called amillennialists. In my opinion, they are taking a dangerous position. They believe we can accept some promises as literal and reject others. They say we cannot interpret literally the promises and covenants of Israel.

God promised to bring Israel back to their land from all corners of the world, and this miracle is literally taking place. Amillennialists believe Israel is returning to the land, yet they still say the promises to Israel are not to be interpreted literally!

God promised Abraham the land of Israel as an everlasting possession. The land of Israel is real! In His Word, God has also promised there will be 1,000 years of peace—a literal number of years. He has promised to cast Satan into the bottomless pit. In fact, He has even revealed the identity of the angel of the bottomless pit: his name is Abbaddon, in the Hebrew, and Apollyon, in the Greek.

When the Bible speaks literally, we must believe it literally. When God makes a promise to us we can take it literally and stand on it. When God said Jesus would come, He fulfilled His promise literally and Jesus was born in Bethlehem. Jesus was literally crucified and He literally rose again. He has promised to literally return for His church and rule and reign on the earth for 1,000 years. If we cannot accept the Millennium as literal, then to be consistent, we cannot interpret the promise of Christ's return as being literal. Neither can we believe in a literal heaven and hell or a literal resurrection.

Just because we do not understand something doesn't mean we must reject it. "Eye hath not seen, nor ear heard, neither have entered into the heart of man, the things which God hath prepared for them that love him" (1 Corinthians 2:9).

God is not going to be defeated by the curse. Satan is not going to defy God's sovereign Word and win. God's covenants with Israel will be kept. The Scriptures will be fulfilled. The Lord will prove to the nations that the only hope for peace is by the direct rule of the Prince of Peace. The curse cannot be removed by any program of man, but only through the rule of Christ.

What Will the Millennium Be Like?

What will life be like during the Millennium? The whole world will be different. The moon will shine as brightly as the sun does now, and the light of the sun will be seven times greater (Isaiah 30:26).

136

Beautiful flowers and luscious fruits and vegetables will grow easily in the rich soil. No longer will there be any weeds or thorns, and the crops will be bountiful.

During Christ's millennial reign, the human, animal, and bird kingdoms will live together without fear. The lion and lamb will lie down together, and the cow and the bear will feed together (Isaiah 11:6-9).

Christ will rule the world from Jerusalem, and the saints will reign with Him. There will be universal peace (Micah 4:3), and all the nations will serve the Lord (Psalm 72:11). Man's life span will be greatly lengthened (Isaiah 65:20), and the glory of the Lord will fill the whole earth.

It is hard for us to grasp the glory of a millennial kingdom. We have become so accustomed to sin, unbelief, and crime. *But we are children of the promise.* We have been born anew by the Spirit of God. We are children of faith.

The truth of the millennial kingdom teaches us that the future of our lives should not be dependent upon the arm of flesh and the wisdom of men. It teaches us that God is in control and His promises can be trusted. But most of all, it teaches us that even now we can come under the gracious rule of our wonderful Lord. Soon the Lord himself will be revealed in physical reality. But even now He is a spiritual reality ruling over His kingdom, calling out a people for His name. If we confess Him now, He promises He will confess us before His Father.

The Bible clearly tells us the time is coming when every knee shall bow before Him and every tongue shall confess that Jesus Christ is Lord. It is incumbent upon us, as Gentiles whom God has blessed, to respond to the revelation of His person and the glory of His truth. Soon the times of the Gentiles will be fulfilled. Now is the time to acknowledge Him as Saviour. Come under His gracious rule now and become a citizen of His eternal kingdom. Then you will share in the millennial kingdom and be part of the first resurrection.

15

Is Hell a Biblical Doctrine or a Sadistic Idea?

The Final Judgment

There will be a final judgment in which the wicked dead will be raised and judged according to their works. Whosoever is not found written in the Book of Life, together with the devil and his angels, the beast and the false prophet, will be consigned to everlasting punishment in the lake which burneth with fire and brimstone, which is the second death (Matthew 25:46; Mark 9:43-48; Revelation 19:20; 20:11-15; 21:8).

Surely every sensitive person would like to be a universalist when it comes to the final judgment. No one in his right mind would desire that another human being come to the end of his life facing the bitter pain of eternal condemnation and everlasting punishment. This is why a belief that assures eternal life and bliss to the soul of every man has such a tremendous attraction. However, sentiment cannot be exalted above the Word of God.

Once, I tried to avoid the subject of hell and the lake of fire. I wanted to make the Scriptures prove the annihilation of the wicked. I examined the doctrine of the restoration of all things and studied the doctrine of purgatory, in order to preach hope for the wicked after death. I wanted to believe that final punishment will be only for a period of time. But to believe and preach these false doctrines would be to deny the literal truth of the Bible. I would have to deny the words of Jesus, Paul, John, and the prophets, and I would have to deny the holiness and justice of the living God.

As a minister of Christ, I am dutybound before the living God to preach the whole truth and nothing but the truth. I must tell people *what God says* and *not what man thinks.* I must tell them the good news of the gospel, but I must also warn them about the consequences of not accepting the gospel.

Let us imagine that a train carrying hundreds of passengers is speeding down the tracks. I have gone ahead of the train and discovered that a section of the trestle over a raging river has fallen. If I am a responsible person, I will immediately think, "I must warn the people on the train in order to save their lives." But some people might say, "You shouldn't do that. You might be seeing things. You might also frighten the passengers, and some of them might faint. Be nice and don't disturb them." No! If I love people, I must lift my voice and warn those on the speeding train of the peril.

The doctrine of the final judgment is the warning bell of God to warn every human of the terrible consequences of ignoring the claims of Jesus Christ. Why does the Church believe and preach the fact of hell and the lake of fire?

Why We Believe in Hell

Jesus, the ultimate authority and teacher of truth, taught the doctrine of eternal punishment.

Vance Havner was once told by a convention committee not to preach on hell and the lake of fire, but to preach instead about the meek and lowly Jesus. Havner responded, "Gentlemen, nearly everything I learned about hell came from the meek and lowly Jesus."

In Matthew 25, at the end of His great Olivet Discourse, Jesus revealed that when the Son of Man comes in His glory, there will be a judgment. He will say to the wicked: "Depart from me, ye cursed, into everlasting fire, prepared for the devil and his angels" (v. 41). And He concluded His great discourse with these awesome words: "And these shall go away into everlasting punishment: but the righteous into life eternal" (v. 46).

In Mark 9:42, Jesus warns His disciples not to offend one of the little ones that believe in Him. Then He makes this bold statement: "It is better for thee to enter into life maimed, than having two hands to go into hell, into the fire that never shall be quenched: where their worm dieth not, and the fire is not quenched" (Mark 9:43,44).

In Luke 13:3, Jesus cries, "Except ye repent, ye shall all likewise perish." Does "perish" mean they'll go to heaven? Of course not! And in John 3:18, He says: "He that believeth on him is not condemned: but he that believeth not is condemned already, because he hath not believed in the name of the only begotten Son of God." Condemned to what? Heaven? No! Men are not condemned to heaven, they are condemned to hell.

Paul believed in hell. Second Thessalonians 1:8,9 says:

In flaming fire taking vengeance on them that know not God, and that obey not the gospel of our Lord Jesus Christ: who shall be punished with everlasting destruction from the presence of the Lord, and from the glory of his power.

John believed in hell. Revelation 14:10 says:

> The same shall drink of the wine of the wrath of God, which is poured out without mixture into the cup of his indignation; and he shall be tormented with fire and brimstone in the presence of the holy angels, and in the presence of the Lamb.

And in Revelation 20:15, John notes: "And whosoever was not found written in the book of life was cast into the lake of fire."

These are but a few of the Scripture passages that clearly show the reality of the existence of hell and the lake of fire, which have been prepared for the devil and his angels. Our church believes this doctrine because it is taught by Christ and the Holy Scriptures.

We believe in eternal punishment because there is a just necessity for punishment.

Underlying every law must be a counteracting consequence. Man is a subject of divine government. Justice requires that man meet certain obligations. When he fails to meet those requirements, it is incumbent upon a righteous government to judge the offender and mete out punishment equal to the crime. The Bible says: "The wages of sin is death" (Romans 6:23); "The soul that sinneth, it shall die" (Ezekiel 18:20); "Be sure your sin will find you out" (Numbers 32:23); and, "Without shedding of blood is no remission [of sin]" (Hebrews 9:22).

In our culture, the preacher must clearly state the consequences of sin. We live in a society that is "soft" on the consequences of wrongdoing. This is to our moral detriment and is a grave danger to our eternal souls. God wants us to have righteous government for one reason: to teach men by example that breaking the law has serious consequences. The powers that be are ordained of God; they are to minister righteousness and justice. God will hold every governor, legislator, judge, and civil authority accountable for their failure to uphold justice and mete out punishment. However, men's failures *do not determine* God's laws. God's laws simply *reveal* men's failures.

We are living in a dangerous time because sin is often not met with a corresponding judgment. However, the person who chooses to die in his sins will face the consequences of his sins in spite of men's failure to punish wrongdoing. God's nature, His character, and His Word demand the execution of judgment upon the ungodly.

Too many mistakenly interpret the long-suffering of God as a cancellation of judgment, when it is only a postponement of judgment. The love of God will soon dictate the need for Him to destroy sin and punish the sinner. Too many disregard the Word of God because men's laws have changed. Too many ignore the Word of God because it appears that many offenders have escaped the judgment of society. There are not enough law enforcement agencies in the world to catch and jail every criminal. Too many offenders are hiding in the crowd, hoping to escape the notice of the judge. But there is no escape from God; men must deal with Him.

Every man's sins must be punished either in Jesus Christ or in the sinner. Those who reject the work of Christ are taking the punishment of sin upon themselves. Those who will not live for Christ and persist in sinning are asking to face God *in rebellion* and not *in repentance.* We are going to be judged by the living God, not by dying men. Men have set up one set of rules, but they are not the rules by which men will be judged at the Great White Throne.

Unrepented sin, which is rebellion against the light, isolates the sinner from the covering of the Blood. It removes him from the mercy of God and places him under God's wrath. The Bible says that all liars will have their part in the lake of fire. Don't try to change it! Don't try to cover it with cosmetics. Face it, if you know you are a liar in your heart and you've tried to excuse it rather than repent and turn from it, you will have your part in the lake of fire. If you don't, God himself is a liar.

The Bible says that unrepented sexual sins destroy the soul, and the consequence is hell and the lake of fire. We could say this isn't so, but it would not be true. The Bible says: "Let God be true, but every man a liar" (Romans 3:4). If you are having sex outside of marriage and do not repent of that sin and turn to the Lord, you will have your part in the lake of fire. If you are living an adulterous life and do not repent, turn to God for mercy, and reject that life-style, you are sealing your doom in the lake of fire. If you are practicing homosexuality and do not repent and reject that life-style, your eternal soul is under the judgment of God, and you will have your part in the lake of fire. If you're a drunkard, you will not inherit the kingdom of God. If you do not repent and reject that life-style, you are holding a false hope if you plan to enter heaven.

First John 3:9 says that whoever is born of God cannot sin. In other words, he cannot live a sinful life-style. He cannot go on rebelling against God.

The Bible says there are people who will return to a life-style of sin, but the latter state is worse for them than the beginning. It would have been better if they had never known. But those who are born of God have a different destiny, and they will not persist in rebellion.

A preacher once preached a sermon on hell. Following the sermon, a woman asked him if he had any children. He replied that he did. "Do you love them?" she asked. "Oh yes," the preacher answered. "Well," the woman said, "what would you think of a father who could save his children from suffering, but refused to do it?" "I would say that he was a tyrant and a monster," replied the preacher. "Then that's what you're making God out to be," she answered. "God would be a monster if He sent His children to hell instead of delivering them by His power."

Then the preacher said, "But, lady, you have made one mistake. God does not have any children in hell, and He never will. The people in hell are the devil's children. All of God's children are in heaven or are on their way there. God has His home for His children, and Satan has his home for his children."

We believe in hell and the lake of fire because heaven would be hell if sin and the sinner were allowed to enter.

Look at what happened to our earth. It was created as a veritable garden, but sin entered, bringing death and the curse of God. God has shown us He cannot allow sin to enter heaven. Only the ransomed and redeemed may enter those pearly gates.

God would not be a merciful God if He did not provide a means to escape the penalty of sin. But He is merciful. He has provided a way of escape. However, if an individual refuses to accept the provision of mercy, then God would not be just if He did not bring that person into judgment.

We have seen the basic reasons why we believe in eternal punishment. Now we will examine the nature of hell and the lake of fire.

What Is Hell Like?

Jesus himself gives us a picture of hell in Luke 16. The account of the rich man and Lazarus begins with the words: "There was a certain rich man, . . . and there was a certain beggar named Lazarus" (Luke 16:19,20). We know Jesus is not speaking in a parable when He identifies certain people and calls them by name. He is pulling aside the curtain to show us Sheol prior to His delivering the souls of just men.

Luke 16:23 reads: "And in hell he [the rich man] lifted up his eyes, being in torments" (Luke 16:23). The word translated "hell" is the word *hades*, the place of departed spirits. Before Christ set the souls of men free from paradise, it was possible to look across a mighty gulf in Sheol that separated paradise from hades. Both those in paradise and those in hades were conscious of each other. Through Christ's resurrection, the paradise of old is empty and, at death, the believer is immediately with the Lord.

We notice several things about hell:

1. Hell is a place of consciousness. The rich man was able to see and recognize Lazarus, whom he had known on earth.

2. Hell is a place of conscious, unending suffering. The Bible says the rich man was in torment to such

an extent that he begged for someone to dip the tip of his finger in water and give him a moment of relief from the terrible heat and flames.

3. Hell is a place of separation. The sinner will be separated from those who are honest and redeemed. But most important, he will be eternally separated from God. There is nothing worse than that. Imagine being abandoned forever; eternally separated from the mercies and love of God! The greatest anguish of the cross was when Jesus felt the temporary separation from His Father because of the sin Jesus was bearing.

4. Hell is a place of regrets and memory. The sinner will remember his loved ones. He will regret his unbelief. He will regret that he influenced others away from God.

5. Hell is a place of prayer. Oh the wailing and crying! Oh the anguish of unanswered prayer. But it will be too late! There will be no returning. There will be no hope. The sinner will be forever lost.

When does this dreadful doctrine take effect? The rebellious sinner and the person who rejects Christ will upon death immediately find themselves in hell. Their bodies will go into the ground, but their souls, their conscious selves, will instantly be in the spirit world. They will be with the rich man—in constant torment.

After the Rapture and the Second Coming, Jesus will set up His millennial kingdom for 1,000 years. After the thousand years, Satan will be loosed for a season to test those who were born during the Millennium. Millions will turn against God and fight the Lord in a final battle. Once and for all, God will pour out His wrath and effect the final judgment. Satan will be cast into the lake of fire with the beast and the false prophet.

Revelation 20:12 reads: "And I saw the dead, small and great, stand before God; and the books were opened." All the unbelieving dead will be resurrected, and in the presence of the Judge of heaven and earth, the secrets of every heart will be revealed. Everything not forgiven or covered by the Blood will be exposed.

In one violent thrust of omnipotent power, God will cast death and hell into the lake of fire, and anyone whose name is not found written in the Book of Life will also be cast into the lake of fire.

It's an awesome thing to realize you could be in hell one minute from now, for there is only a step between you and death. It is a certain fact that after death comes the judgment.

A brave man was dying. His friend said to him, "Are you afraid of dying?" "Oh no," the man answered, "I have faced death many times. But it is what follows death that is driving me crazy."

How can we face God? By accepting His great salvation. Open the books of your life *now* and examine yourself. Is it a record of sin? Are the pages full of self and sin? Face it now! Are you able to stand before God at this moment? If the answer is "no," repent—or perish. Cry out to God for mercy in Jesus' name. Turn from sin, and embrace your Saviour. Stand before God in Jesus' name. Your sins may be black, but your Saviour is able to forgive and cleanse from all unrighteousness. God is calling you now. Don't postpone this important matter. Don't take the risk!

General Booth was speaking to a group of cadets in the Salvation Army. "Young men," he said, "if I had my way, I would not put you through this training. But I would put you in hell for 24 hours. I would allow you to feel the pain, the pangs of the doomed; hear the weeping and wailing and the gnashing of teeth. Then I would send you out into the world to warn men to flee from the wrath to come." (Quoted from *Simple Sermons on Heaven, Hell, and Judgment,* by W. Herschel Ford [Grand Rapids: Zondervan Publishing House, 1969], p. 68.)

Thank God it's not too late! Dr. Scarborough preached one night on the rich man and Lazarus. An unsaved man heard the sermon. Later, the man went home, but he could not sleep. His wife asked, "What's the matter?" He answered, "Is it true what the preacher said about being separated in eternity?" His wife got her Bible and read the words, ". . . between us and you there is a great gulf fixed" (Luke 16:26). The man said, "We've never been separated since we married. I don't want to be separated in eternity. Pray for me, I want to receive Christ." He was saved that night. The next Sunday he walked down the aisle and grasped Dr. Scarborough's hand and said, "Preacher, the other night I got on my wife's side of the great gulf!" (Taken from *Simple Sermons on Heaven, Hell, and Judgment,* by W. Herschel Ford [Grand Rapids: Zondervan Publishing House, 1969], p. 57.)

If you died tonight, on which side of the gulf would you find yourself?

16

Good Heavens! It's Real!

The New Heavens and the New Earth

"We, according to his promise, look for new heavens and a new earth wherein dwelleth righteousness" (2 Peter 3:13; Revelation 21; 22).

The Christian is the only person on earth who can logically rejoice in the past, present, and future. The problem of the past has been solved by the Blood. The problem of the present is solved by the power of the Holy Spirit. The problem of the future will be solved by the reality of an eternal home called heaven.

Biblical doctrines are impossible for the carnal mind to entertain, let alone understand. Scriptural truth is spiritually discerned. If a person chooses not to believe, he chooses not to participate in the kingdom of God. He that cometh to God must believe. Our statements of faith are declarations of faith. Even if we do not understand them completely, we live by them because we believe in Him whom God sent to reveal truth.

Our fundamental reason for believing in a literal heaven is the same as our reason for believing every other doctrine: Jesus taught it, the Scriptures declare it, and we accept it. Jesus himself promised us eternal life. Any schoolboy knows eternity means "unending." Jesus said: "Whosoever liveth and believeth in me shall never die" (John 11:26). We will never cease to exist. There should be no argument about the fact of eternal life through Christ. The declaration of John 3:16 clarifies it: ". . . that whosoever believeth in him should not perish, but have everlasting life."

If we are going to live forever, it is obvious we are going to live somewhere. The Bible does not leave us in doubt concerning this. The unbelieving sinner will live forever in the lake of fire. The believing Christian will be forever with the Lord. If someone should ask you, "Where will you spend eternity?" if you are a born-again Christian, your answer should be, "With Jesus."

The apostle Paul knew this. In his letter to the church at Philippi, he shared a dilemma that he faced. He was really between a rock and a hard place! He wanted to die, yet he also wanted to live. From Paul's point of view, it would be far better to die because He would be with the Lord. However, it would be better for the Philippians if he lived (Philippians 1:21-24).

Can We Believe It?

If we will be with Jesus, it is logical then to ask, "Where is Jesus, and where will He spend the future?" If we answer these questions, then we will know where we will live forever.

Again, the Scriptures leave us no doubt. Jesus is now at the throne of God in heaven. He will rule and reign on the earth for 1,000 years, after which the throne of God will be with men in the new heavens and the new earth.

Jesus verified this truth for us in John 14:1-3:

Let not your heart be troubled. . . . In my Father's house are many mansions: If it were not so, I would have told you. I go to prepare a place for you. And if I go and prepare a place for you, I will come again, and receive you unto myself; that where I am, there ye may be also.

Jesus also urged: "Lay up for yourselves treasures in heaven, where neither moth nor rust doth corrupt, and where thieves do not break through nor steal" (Matthew 6:20). He promised eternal rewards to those who are faithful.

Why do we believe in heaven? Because the Boss has told us about it. Heaven is a real place. The glorious description given in the Book of Revelation confirms some of the details, which are almost too wondrous and glorious for the human tongue to tell. Jesus said He would prepare a *place* for us—not an attitude of the mind; not a symbol; but a *place*. We should not be surprised at the capability of our Lord to prepare an eternal and glorious residence for us.

If the contractor who built the house you are now living in contracts to build you another house, you would have no doubt that he can fulfill the contract because he has done it before. Those who say, "I can't believe in heaven," are terribly illogical. The One who took the contract to build a new heaven and a new earth, also built the present one.

The present heavens declare the glory of God. Show me someone who could duplicate this universe we're living in, and I will believe he could duplicate the new heavens, the new earth, and the New Jerusalem, which are so graphically described for us in the Bible. The present world is enough to stagger our imagination. The things the eye can see and the ear can hear are real. But when scientists describe this universe to me, I have to accept it by faith because my eye has not seen, nor my ear heard, the things that scientists have discovered through their faith and understanding of the universe.

If you think heaven is hard to believe, you should try to believe what the astronomers tell us. They say this planet is spinning like a top in space, and that it continually circles the sun, which is 93 million miles away. They also state that the moon, while reflecting light from the sun, travels around the earth at an average distance of 238,000 miles. Furthermore, they report that if the moon were to get off its course by just a few inches, it would send a massive tidal wave over the whole earth!

Scientists estimate that the sun is so big that if we could hollow it out, there would be enough space to put the earth in the center and still have enough room left inside for the moon to maintain its same orbit around the earth. They also believe that if the sun were to cool down just 3 degrees in temperature, the earth's oceans would freeze like a block of ice.

Astronomers say the nearest star is 26 trillion miles from earth. That's 4 light-years away! Light travels at 186,000 miles per second, or almost 12 billion miles a minute. Traveling at that speed, it would take 4 years to reach the next star. According to astronomers, our galaxy contains approximately 100 billion stars, and it would take a beam of light 100,000 years to travel from one end of our galaxy to the other (traveling at 186,000 miles per second). Furthermore, our galaxy is just one of many in the universe!

Scientists want us to believe all that! It's hard for

me to believe them, but I do. Yet, some of these people say in the same breath that we're crazy to believe something as "far out" as heaven!

New Heavens and a New Earth

Christ created this incredible world and universe, and has held it together through all time by the power of His Word. We can believe Him above any scientist. Heaven is not only real, but also *near*.

In 2 Peter 3:10-13 we are informed of the coming eternal state. Peter also prophesies that scoffers will come in the last days, saying, "Where is the promise of his coming?" (2 Peter 3:3,4).

But Jesus will come. This is the blessed hope. Our bodies will be changed into glorified bodies. We will come back with Jesus for the millennial reign. After the Millennium, Satan will be loosed for a season, and the final struggle against Christ will be waged. Satan and his hordes will be cast into the lake of fire. All the dead will stand before the Throne, and those whose names are not written in the Book of Life will be cast into the lake of fire. Then the old earth and the old heaven will be completely transformed. A new birth for the earth will take place; literally, *palingensia*. The light source for the new heaven and new earth will be the Shekinah glory of God. The former things will pass away.

But the apostle John tells us we are to look for not just a new heaven and a new earth, but also the New Jerusalem, the new capital of the eternal universe. "And I John saw the holy city, New Jerusalem, coming down from God out of heaven, prepared as a bride adorned for her husband" (Revelation 21:2).

God's purpose for mankind is to glorify God and

to establish an eternal relationship with Him. Sin made that impossible for a time, but God will not be defeated in His divine purpose. He has made us new; He has already given us a new birth by the Spirit. He is going to do the same thing for this old world. The present heaven and earth will be reborn by fire to make room for the eternal state.

The Bible tells us that the "things which are seen were not made of things which do appear" (Hebrews 11:3). *Visibility is not essential to reality.* The things we see are not the essence of reality. The eternal is the essence of the invisible. Now, we are not equipped to see that which is real and eternal, but someday we shall be like Jesus. We will see Him, and we will be able to grasp the eternal. We will realize then that the earth has been only a temporary way station, and reality has been the things of the Spirit.

Picture our earth completely reborn with no trace of sin, the curse, or the disharmony of nature. Think of our sun, moon, and stars fleeing away. After all, He who called the solar and lunar lights into existence can replace them with something better; the earth will be alight with the Holy Spirit. The New Jerusalem, in all of its magnificence, will take its place in God's promised plan.

The New Jerusalem

In Revelation 21 and 22, John tries to describe the dimensions and character of the city. It is hard to imagine the difficulty John had in attempting to describe the indescribable.

I have always enjoyed the story of the little child who was born blind. There seemed to be no hope that she would ever see, until a famous surgeon developed a surgical technique that would correct the problem that had caused the child's blindness. On the fateful day, the final bandages were removed. For the first time in the child's life, she was able to see her parents. She looked and looked at them, drinking in every detail of their faces. After a long period of time, she was attracted to the window. For the first time in her life she had the joy of seeing sunlight, trees, and houses. Turning away from the window, she finally said, "Mother, why didn't you tell me it was so beautiful?" The mother replied with deep emotion, "Darling, I tried, but I just couldn't get the job done."

I believe the children of God will spend considerable time in eternity just looking at Jesus, and then they will take a look at heaven and ask the same question of John the apostle: "Why didn't you tell us it was so beautiful?" Well, he tried, but there was no way he could get the job done.

According to John's description of heaven, the capital of the universe will be 1,500 miles square. Can you picture a city approximately two-thirds the size of the continental United States? Around the entire perimeter will be a foundation of 12 different stones, symbolizing the 12 apostles whose message of Christ is the foundation of eternal glory. The foundation will be adorned with all kinds of beautiful jewels. Abraham looked for this city. He saw it by faith, and one day he will see it in reality.

On top of the foundation, around the perimeter of the city, will stand a wall "great and high," made of what John describes as jasper, which will allow light to pass through (Revelation 21:12,18). Imagine approaching the New Jerusalem with its bejeweled foundations and its massive walls that radiate light!

On each side of the city, there will be three massive entrances with gates of pearl. Each gate will be formed by a single pearl, which reminds us of Jesus, the Pearl of Great Price, who gave so much and suffered to create beauty out of ashes. His suffering makes entrance into the city possible. Doors will be on each side of the city, because salvation is for all, and the gates will always be open. There will be no need to keep the gates closed because there will be no sin in the universe.

The city will be not only 1,500 miles square, but also 1,500 miles high—possibly in the shape of a pyramid, with terraced balconies for eternal residences. Someone with unusual curiosity has attempted to show that the New Jerusalem could house 53 billion people in that 1,500-square-mile city. There will be plenty of room. Jesus himself said His Father's house has many mansions.

No one can imagine the throne of God, although Ezekiel and John both tried to describe it. It will be a throne of light, as a "sardine stone," with a rainbow around it and a sea of crystal glass before its steps (Ezekiel 1:26-28; Revelation 4:2-6). Four great beasts will bow in praise, and the energy emanating from the throne will be incredible. Flowing from the throne will be the pure river of the water of life, clear as crystal. Revelation 22:2 describes the river as flowing down the center of a mighty boulevard, with trees of healing on either side of it. The trees will bear 12 types of fruit, one for each month.

Since there will be no sickness there, some have questioned the need for the trees' leaves of healing for the nations. The Greek word used is *therapeia*, meaning "health giving." The leaves will have a therapeutic effect, providing invigoration and exhilaration rather than healing from a disease. So when you need to be invigorated, you'll pluck a leaf!

A Heavenly Home

More than just a place, heaven will be *home,* our eternal home. We are going to have a perfect home in a perfect place. A home is a place of permanence. This world is not our home because it is always changing and restless. It is like a restless sea, but there will be no sea like that in heaven.

We will have permanent bodies. We will be like Jesus after He rose from the dead and His earthly body was glorified. Our body structure will be such that we will know each other. That is why spiritual fellowship is part of the treasures laid up forever. We will be as the angels, in that we will not marry, be given in marriage, or procreate. No part of our bodies will be subject to disease, and God himself shall wipe away everything that has ever brought tears to our eyes.

Our relationships in heaven will be perfect. There will be no more sins to separate us from God or one another. No longer will pride tempt us to rebel against God. There will be no more hurt feelings because there will be perfect understanding of motives, and there will be no more jealousy. Every trace of sin, uncleanliness, sorrow, and dying will be forever put away, "for the former things are passed away" (Revelation 21:4).

The Bible says God's servants will serve Him day and night. Work will be done in heaven, but no labor. There will be activity and fulfillment, but no more drudgery and futility. It will be a world of perfection.

How can you go there? First, by desiring a better world and recognizing, by the help of the Spirit, that this world is no longer your permanent home. You must begin to live by faith, rejecting sin and accepting Jesus. You must see the world you are in and the life you are living as inadequate. God made you for more than this world.

A crane was eating snails when a swan appeared near him. "Where did you come from?" asked the crane. "From heaven," replied the swan. "What's it like?" "Oh, it's beautiful beyond description—a land of absolute love and perfection." "Do they have snails there?" questioned the crane. "No snails," said the swan, "but there are far better things." "Oh then," said the crane, "I can't think of going to a place that doesn't have snails."

Stop looking for snails! Look up, lift up your head, and rejoice, for your redemption is drawing near. When the desire for heaven grips your soul, the next step is to obtain a reservation. There is only one who can authorize your reservation; there is no other name with the authority to prepare a place for you. Believe on the Lord Jesus Christ and you will have your reservation. How? By being born again spiritually. You were born once and that made you earthbound, so naturally you went the way of sin. But Christ came to give you new birth by the Spirit, to make you part of Him. He is the entrance to eternal life.

The following story may be a legend, but it is beautiful. One day, a handsome prince told his father, the king, that he was afraid of marrying because he could not be sure that he could find someone who would love him for himself and not just for the prestige and wealth he could offer. The king said, "The only way you can be sure is to disguise yourself as a poor man." So the prince disguised himself as a farmhand, and traveled to the furthest region of the kingdom.

Soon he fell in love with a farmer's daughter. The farmer would not put up with it, but love prevailed, and the couple was married in spite of the farmer's rage. The disguised prince said to his young bride, "I have a surprise for you. We are going on a honeymoon." The bride was rather surprised that her husband could afford a honeymoon of any kind. After all, he was just a poor farmhand.

They traveled to the capital city and arrived at the palace gates. A nod of recognition was given, and to the amazement of the little farm girl, the gates swung open, the trumpets blared, and the king himself came forward to greet them. In absolute shock, the young bride turned to her new husband and asked the obvious question, "What is this all about?" "My dear," said the prince, "you married me in obscurity, which proved you loved me. Now all the honors and benefits of the realm are yours."

My friend, Jesus of Nazareth was despised and rejected. He disguised himself as a lowly servant, but He was, in reality, the King of kings. Those who now confess Him out of love are often mocked for wasting their time and effort on one so simple and obscure. But someday this Man with the sandaled feet will reveal who He is to the whole world. I pray that the Holy Spirit will reveal to you who He is now, so you can spend eternity with Him in heaven. If you will confess Him before men, He will confess you before His Father, and all the honor and benefits of the heavenly realm will be yours.